Dancing

Guide

DANCING GUIDE

BASIC ART OF THE DANCE

Ballroom	Latin	Disco
Country	Line	Latino

John Amos Banks

Library of Congress Catalog Card Number 99-94028

ISBN   0-9629833-2-2

Published by
Jordan Book Company
8434 Keller Road
Panama City, FL 32404

Preface

Dancing is the oldest of the fine arts and it extends back to primitive times when our ancestors were still hairy. These folks would go out and kill a boar for supper, bring it back to the village and then celebrate by dancing around a campfire. It is not likely that they danced the waltz or tango but it is certain that people never stopped dancing from that early day to the present day.

And one aspect of the dance has not changed since those ancient times and that is the fact that dancing has two major parts, namely, gaining the ability to dance and then performing the dance in an artful manner.

Gaining the ability to dance requires a firm will to achieve the goal of being a dancer and a hard discipline of learning and practice. This is not easy to do but there is fun in the learning and a joy of achieving.

Performing a dance is to exhibit the skill that has been learned. Here one expresses the beautiful art of dancing, either for a self-enjoyment alone or for a public appreciation. The skill forms the foundation while the performance, the actual dancing, exhibits that skill as art and that is the pinnacle of dancing.

How does one gain this skill in order to become an artful dancer? There is only one known way to do this and that is by learning and practice: first learn the skill so that a store of knowledge is banked in the mind and then practice, practice, practice so that an expertness is banked in the muscles. And of course this is true whether one wishes to become a dancer, a musician, a surgeon or a good housewife.

The prime purpose of this book is to instruct in the skill of dancing, in the foundation of the art of dancing. Once the skill has been acquired it remains only to exhibit that skill in an artistic manner.   Can one acquire this skill merely by reading a book and without the aid of a teacher? Yes, but to a very limited degree.   Instruction by a dance teacher is indispensable if one expects to acquire the title of "good dancer" or artistic dancer. The groundwork and a modest skill of dancing can be learned alone but   an instructor will ice the cake with art.

In this book we have presented the skill of dancing in a method quite different from that which is found in most dance books.   Rather than scatter the information for each dance across a half dozen pages, we have condensed the same data into a table format which is the modern way of instruction. Each dance is described in a compact, a concise manner, making it easier to read, easier to absorb the information. The pattern of steps and the rhythm count can be seen and followed without leafing back and forth in the book.   Just hold the book open to the proper page for the tango, the waltz, etc, and do the necessary practice.

Specific acknowledgments are not in order. Many books have been perused across the years such as Fred Astaire, Vernon Castle, Arthur Murray, Lustgarten, Laird, Sylvester, Wright, etc., and their wisdom sub-consciously retained, but the system of presentation, (the ten-part pattern) is original with the author.

This is a guide book that points the way, only you alone or with the help of a teacher, can develop the skill of dancing and the art of the dance. We hope you do so. From the stone age of the barbarians, to primitive man, to civilized man and down to modern times, dancing has been the one form of personal and social recreation that has endured. It has endured with the high and the low, the rich and the poor, the healthy and the ill. Don't hesitate to join the rest of humanity in this beneficial form of healthful and social recreation. It will relieve the stresses of life and brighten your daily living.

CONTENTS

Introduction

DANCING - THE GREATEST ART

We cannot discuss dancing intelligently until we have first considered the nature of art itself for dancing is, after all, one of the fine arts. Moreover, if we have a clear image of the nature of art then we shall better understand dancing as an art and as a skillful action.

Art is a human behavior that is devoted to the production of beautiful and useful objects. We know these objects as pictures, music, building structures, and craft products, objects that have been created with graceful contours, and space areas that are pleasing to the eye and useful in human living. Thus art is not confined to what is called "the fine arts" only, but extends throughout all of life , both human and in nature. Houses, automobiles, clothing, man-made landscapes and gardens are all products of artful production. And nature produces its own artful objects of sunset and sunrise, pretty flowers and majestic mountains.

An object contains the quality of art because it has a value: it is a desired thing, a preferred thing, a good thing that evokes pleasure in the human mind. There are many pictures in the world and much music but only certain pictures and certain musical pieces "have" art, (are artful) because they are desirable, are pleasant to see or hear. In other words they have beauty in their presence, they give pleasure and therefore are works of art, not crude objects.

The arts have been grouped (by Zimmerman) into three classes:

1) Arts that represent material things: sculpture, architecture, (craft objects), etc.;

2) Arts that have perceptive representation: painting, music, etc.;

3) Arts that represent thought: reasoning, poetry, literature.

DANCING - THE PECULIAR ART

You will have observed that dancing is not included in the above list and there is a very special reason for this because dancing stands alone, is a category of art unlike any other, and this comes about in the following way.

We said in the beginning that art is devoted to the production of objects. But dancing does not produce an object. Once the dance is performed it is over and done with, no product remains. The dancer who does the dance IS THE ART, is the product, by his or her movements. Unlike painting, surgery, sculpture and music, which are performed by an artist and leave a product to behold, dancing leaves no product, the dance itself, as it is being performed, is the end product. Once the dance is performed, whether by a child, a bear, ballet dancer or a folk dancer, it is gone forever (unless recorded on a tape). It is the human body that is the mold, the action and the end product.

Thus dancing is a peculiar art unto itself, unlike all other arts. This has no particular significance. It is set aside as the great art because of its unusual nature and because every human being "does" this art sometime during their lifetime.

THE THREE PRIME PARTS OF DANCING

To produce his art the painter will have his brushes, the musician his horn and the sculptor his model as tools of their art but the dancer has only his body as a tool to produce his art. Therefore, he must devise a way to use this body-tool and he does so in three particular ways: by acquiring a body skill, which he does by practice; by mating his skill with musical sounds; and, by performing a set of dance patterns.

1. The Body Skills of Dancing.

Body skill means an ability: to walk, to run, jump, move forward and backward, pivot in a circle. In dancing, these skills must be done with agility and usually in unison with another person, that is, with a dance partner. The skilled ability includes also a proficiency, an expertness to perform body movements and in dancing it means to perfom these motions with graceful movements.

The only known way to gain or acquire this skill is by learning the dance patterns and then to practice, practice, practice. And of course this is true whether the goal is dancing, sports, brain surgery or business administration.

2. Mating the Body Skill with Music.

Dance patterns can be performed merely by walking through the figures but this is not true dancing. To dance there must be a pattern of steps that are taken in time to the rhythm, to the beat of music so that the movements flow and progress in an order, in a systematic way, in a continuous stream of motion. The waltz, the foxtrot and ballet would be a dry run of action without a musical beat to control the series of steps.

3. Performing a Set of Dance Patterns.

All true dancing has a structure, a patterned way of

moving about on the dance floor. It is a pattern of steps that make a waltz a waltz and not a foxtrot, and a certain design of steps that make a tango a tango and not a cha cha. This pattern of steps is a framework of the skill that has been learned. We see a child "dancing" on the living room floor and a bear "dancing" at the circus but in reality these actions are not a dance, they are merely a hopping up and down with music as a background. The child and the bear do not step to the rhythm of music, they do not dance in an ordered pattern, their dancing is not creative, their torso, arms and legs are not curved into postures that express beauty and grace, and their movements do not convey a sensuous image and flow of life. In other words the child and the bear have no art in their dance because they have no structure in it, no talent expressing art. And it is such skill that is the prelude to artful dancing in the dance hall, the ballroom and the theater.

The Rhythm of the Dance.

We must ever remember that all of life proceeds in a rhythmic pattern: the beating of the heart, the ocean tides, the seasons of the year, the bearing of fruit on the apple tree, the nine-month incubatioin of the new-born, the cycle of child-youth-adult -death.

In dancing, the rhythm consits in a grouping of musical notes clustered into bars, into measures. As the drummer and bass violinist play these notes, a constant, steady beat is produced. And the dancer on the floor steps his or her feet to the accompaniment of this beat. The dance is performed not to the melody of the piano, guitar, saxaphone or trumpet, but to the recurring beat of the drum or other bass instrument.

In the following chapters these three prime elements of the dance: body skill, music in the dance and dance patterns will be discussed.

PART I

ELEMENTS OF THE DANCE

* * *

The essential meaning of the term "to dance" is the movement of the feet and body forward, backward and to the side, in a rhythmic pattern, but beyond this dancing also includes such behavior as social relations, mental concentration and harmony of association with other persons. It is a multiple conduct of personal and social activity from which one receives pleasure and joy.

The elements that makeup this social activity will be discussed in this section under the titles of:

The Meaning of Dancing;

Music and Dancing;

The Dance Pattern;

The Learning Process;

Positions, Steps and Turns

The Categories of Dancing.

Chapter 1

The Meaning of Dancing

In a narrow sense dancing is an active bodily movement on a dance floor done to the accompaniment of musical sound. But the act of dancing involves the whole personality of the person. We shall plumb this whole to discover the full meaning of dancing.

MENTAL ATTITUDE IN DANCING

Above all, dancing is a voluntary action. We are not forced to dance, the law does not require us to dance and unless our own will drives us to do it, it is not necessary to dance. So we approach and enter into the act of dancing with a personal will and wish, a desire to engage in a behavior that we know is pleasing and joyful. Secondly, there is usually an inner drive, a strong desire that is inspired by a feeling of wanting to dance, to move about, to accompany the beat of the music we hear, to express outwardly a feeling that we have within.

But we must have more than just a feeling of wanting to dance. As every dancer knows, dancing is a difficult chore that requires mental concentration and hard physical effort to learn the step patterns, so it requires a positive attitude, a strong determination to succeed in becoming a dancer. The routine of learning and then dancing as an average or good dancer is sometimes discouraging but the process is necessary.

Mental attitude, then, is an important part of dancing. The lack of a positive attention or a firm will can greatly lessen the pleasure, the fun of dancing.

A PATTERN OF STEPS

Every type of dance has its own pattern of steps. The waltz has one pattern, the swing another and the polka its own pattern.   About 90% of the physical act of dancing is a moving of the feet across the dance floor and the other 10% is body and arm movement.

In a large sense dancing is a special form of walking that is embellished   with   varying speeds, changing directions quickly and a time duration of the steps. The speed varies according to the tempo of the music, (beats per minute), directions change to left, right, forward or backward and the time duration of the steps is designated as slow, or quick.

According to the type of dance, some steps have a special format. For example, there is a triple step in the swing (three steps in two beats),   the crossing of one foot over the other in a side step, a kick step and a pivot step.   In addition there are turns and spins and movement of the arms and torso that give artistic expression.

This variety of step patterns   expand the horizons of dancing.

A MARRIAGE OF MUSIC AND BODY MOVEMENT

Music and dancing are inseparable.   As the music is being played in a rhythmic pattern of beats, the feet are moved in a pattern of steps--forward, backward and to the side--that coordinate with the music while the body turns and sways in a like rhythm.   The step patterns, repeated over and over in a serial fashion we know as a waltz, a tango or a ballet.

A VARIETY OF DANCES

The categories of dances is given in Chapter 6 and need only a few examples here.
Theater Dances -   ballet and dramatic dancing.
Ballroom and Latin - Swing and Tango.
Line Dancing - Dancers are in a line, without partners.
Square Dancing - Once a rural dance now popular with "city folks."
Country and Western Dancing - Includes the two-step, ballroom and Latin steps. Cowboy togs enhance the dance.
Disco - danced alone with much body contortions.
Strict Latin (Latino) - Mambo and meringue type dances.

A LEVEL OF DANCING

Three levels of dancing skills are generally recognized. In social dancing a person is commonly   graded as good, moderate (fair) or poor, according to the ability displayed.   In competition dancing, where a person must be expert to even enter, three categories are stated:
Gold, the most talented;
Silver, very good but lacking the final touches of the dance;
Bronze, a skilled dancer.
These levels combined are called the "metallic dances." The good social dancer in any ballroom is dancing in the Bronze class.
In addition to the above there is also the theatrical dances of ballet and drama dancing.

AN ART EXPRESSION

In that branch of philosophy called axiology, which deals with the value of things, (meaning value to human living), dancing is classified as an art. It is the using of the body to express grace and beauty. As an art, dancing is expressed in two ways, as a social engagement and as a fine art expression.

The Social Engagement. This takes place in the ballroom or dance hall as the dancer associates with other dancers and, in particular, one's dance partner. It is an association where public and personal etiquette is exhibited, with finesse, with conversation and in dance floor behavior.

Sociologists call this form of dancing a recreational engagement in the sense that it is not high art, not a theatrical performance. We dance for self-entertainment and for the enjoyment of a skilled achievement, for pleasure.

A Fine Art Expression. In this case one person, or two persons as partners, perform skilled movements with their feet, torso and arms as a dance progresses in unison to the beat of music. It is a graceful and coordinated movement that depicts charm, undulated motion and a use of the body to depict beauty and joy or pathos and suffering.

A HEALTH BENEFIT

Any action of the body is either a health benefit or a health deterrent. Dancing is a powerful benefit.

Now the body does not care a fig about footwork, artistic movement of the limbs and torso or about art expression, it knows only two things: health and illness. One important way that the body gains health is by exercise and if dancing is anything it is certainly exercise In fact, exercise is one-third of all body health, the other two are food and rest.

There is also an intellectual benefit in which one is required to think, to concentrate on the maneuvering to be done and then to remember the sequence of the dance steps. So the mind also benefits from dancing.

Perhaps the capstone of all benefits of dancing is the emotional part. We live in a world that produces in our mind much fuss, strain, striving and stress. In dancing we find a great let-down from this pressure of the emotions. The worries of the world are literally trampled under one's feet! Here we experience the feelings of contentment, enjoyment, enthusiasm and exuberance. Even if one is a poor dancer, the body does not know this, it only recognizes the exercise, a health benefit.

Thus dancing means many things both great and small. It is a skill of the body, a talent of performing, a freedom from worry and stress. Dancing is not only FOR everyone -- everyone NEEDS to dance and experience the joy of it.

Chapter 2

Music and Dancing

Music and dancing are something like the puzzle of the chicken and the egg--which came first?   Did our hairy ancestors slay a hippopotamus for supper and then begin to dance or did they clap their hands first for a musical rhythm and then start to dance?   We'll never know for sure but that's about when music and dancing both began, back in the stone age.

In one sense music and dancing are strange bedfellows. Dancing is really 150 pounds of flesh hopping around on a dance floor while music is a structure of melodic sounds, of tones and rhythm. The body is a living organism, a biological thing while music is a part of science, of physics, of wave motions. But when heard in the dance hall the music inspires the dancer to exhibit the body in a high art, with beauty and proportion, and in the spectator it evokes a feeling of inspired appreciation. The poet says it best: Music and dancing doth sooth the savage soul.

In this small book we cannot discuss music in detail but we must include a brief discussion   of how music and dancing relate, for   they are the prime parts of dancing.

Basically, music is a sound.   And of course so is plain noise, like the engine of an automobile or a baby crying. That which distinguishes music from plain noise consists in four elements: pitch, dynamics (loud or soft), tone color and rhythm.

We are most interested in rhythm because that is the part of music that affects dancing so dramatically, and so we give only a dictionary description of the other three elements.

PITCH

Pitch is the relative highness or lowness of a sound. A man speaks in a lower pitch than a woman because his voice is "pitched" lower.   On the music scale, C has a lower pitch than F.

The cause of variation in the pitch of music is vibrations of the air waves. If you strike the highest key on a piano it will cause a frequency tone of 4,000 cycles per second; if you strike the lowest key on a piano it will cause a frequency of 27 cycle per second.

DYNAMICS

Dynamics refers to the degree of loudness or softness of musical sound. It means the amplitude of the sound. Italian words express this loudness/softness in these words: *pianisssimo* (very soft), *mezza forte* (moderately loud), *fortissimo* (very loud).

TONE COLOR

This is the quality of sound that gives it tone color or timbre, such as bright, mellow, rich, dull, monotonous.

RHYTHM

This is the part of music that so forcefully affects dancing. As we have stated before, all of life is marked by a rhythmic flow: of 60 seconds every hour; of seasons that are cold,warm and then cold again; of growth and decay in all living things.

In music, rhythm consists in four ingredients: beats, meter, accent and tempo. We shall consider these in order.

BEAT

Beat is a unit of time by which notes of music are measured. The beat in *Tiger Rag* is quite fast (occurs frequently), while the beat in *Home On the Range* is slow (occurs at longer intervals).

Every musical piece has its pattern of beats and thus every dance (tango, polka, waltz) has its frequency of steps, either slow, moderate or fast. And here we touch the key relationship between music and dancing because the feet of the dancer are moved about on the floor according to the musical beat, according to the time (frequency) of the beat. As you will note in the description of the dances, the placement of the feet is made according to the beat of music, are lifted up and put back down according to the beat.

We cannot over-emphasize the importance of beat in dancing. Notice in each of the dance descriptions that the second and third columns in each table are headed "rhythmic count" and "step time." These define the beat of the music and the step interval. The music proceeds-is counted as-1, 2, 3 and the steps follow in unison as quick, slow, quick Thus:.

	Ma -ry	had	a	lit-tle	lamb,	lit-tle	lamb,	lit-tle	lamb
Rhythm Count	1	2	3	&	1 2	3 &	1 2	3 &	1 2	3 &
Step Count	Q	Q	Q	Q	Q Q	S	Q Q	S	Q Q	S

All dancing is coordinated with music in this fashion and of all of the "secrets of dancing," this is the most important one. When the dancer's steps of fast and slow match the rhythm count of 1 & 2-that's dancing!

METER

Beats are arranged into groups, are organized into uniform clusters such as 1, 2, 3 in the waltz and 1, 2; 1, 2; 1, 2, in the polka. This organization of beats into uniform groups is called *meter.*
Dance meters are as follows:
Duple meter (the polka) is 2/4 time;
Triple meter, (the waltz) is 3/4 time;
Quadruple meter, 4/4 time, regulates the swing, tango, foxtrot, etc.

ACCENT

Accent refers to placing stress on particular notes. Notes are accented by being played louder or longer than other notes.

TEMPO

Tempo refers to the speed of the beat, the rapidity of the beats. If the tempo is fast then the placement of the foot will be fast; if the   speed is slow then the dance steps will be executed slowly.

AMERICAN DANCE MUSIC

A simple division of American dance music may be given as Folk Music and Jazz Music   but there are many symphonic.pieces written by American composers such as George Gershwin.

FOLK MUSIC

From Colonial Times down to about 1900, American dance

music consisted of the melodies played at fairs, carnivals, parties and "gatherings."   These were lively tunes and the dancing was lively too, such as the square dance, the country round dance, partner dancing and much of it is retained yet today in the "country and western" dances. The city folks and well-to-do danced in ballrooms with the waltz and quadrille. Folk music and dancing continue today but the great popular dances are performed to the beat and melodies of jazz music.

THE BEGINNING OF JAZZ MUSIC

Jazz is not a single kind or type of music, not a single pattern of steps, rather it is a style of music, a category that is distinctly American. It was not written originally to a music scale, which is the usual way to construct a musical theme such as the waltz, rather it "just grew" out of the "soul of the people" as they sang of pity, sorrow, work and also the joy of living.

The ultimate source of jazz music is usually credited to the black musicians of the south, especially New Orleans, where they played instruments in the street, bars, dance hall and bawdy houses. At least this is where jazz first came to public attention about 1910.   These musicians, though direct descendants of black slaves from Africa, were strongly influenced by the white environment in which they lived and by American traditions such as folk tunes, dances, popular songs, native music and hymns. New Orleans was strongly French in mood and manner in the 1890's and this also influenced the attitude of the black musicians. Then, too, this was the age of the American Band when every town and hamlet had its band for parades and park concerts.

Thus the roots of jazz are deep in New Orleans folkways and particularly Storyville, the red-light district of the city that housed saloons, dance halls, gambling joints and girls-for-hire.

When the Navy closed Storyville in 1917 many of the musicians left for Chicago, Kansas City and New York, spreading the sound of jazz to these distant places.

TYPES OF JAZZ MUSIC

One great distinguishing feature of jazz from other styles of music is improvisation. To improvise means to branch off from the main stream (or theme) of a tune and to insert a series of parallel notes that are not written into the music but nevertheless blend into the music in a melodic way, in a harmonic way. These improvised runs are "invented" on the spot, are improvised at the will of the musician.

Jazz is also distinguished by a syncopated rhythm, a progression of strong beats that give emphasis and of tones that are bright and rich.

One other aspect of jazz that is distinctly West African is known as "call-and-response." This is exhibited in several ways. In one, a voice sings and another voice mimics the first voice in a harmonic response. Or, a voice sings and an instrument answers the voice. Or, one instrument is played in the background while another instrument answers with a corresponding note of melody. Call-and-response is widely used in American church services as the audience responds to the preachers call.

RAGTIME. This music was popular from about 1890 to 1915. Ragtime was probably the first type of jazz to be distinguished as a particular pattern. Scott Joplin, the son of a slave who died in 1915, was a composer and pianist and wrote the famous *Maple Leaf Rag.*

THE BLUES. This type of jazz music grew out of black folk music, work songs, spirituals and the talk of field slaves. Blues originated in the late 19th century and came to public attention as a style of music about 1910. Two well known blues pieces are *St. Louis Blues and Memphis Blues* written by the black composer W. C. Handy.

NEW ORLEANS JAZZ. (Also called Dixieland Jazz). This is a style of jazz that developed during the years 1900 to 1916 in several cities but is designated "New Orleans Jazz" because this was the home ground of such famous bands as "Jelly Roll" Morton, King Oliver and his Creole Jazz Band, Louis Armstrong, who played "the blues."

These early bands all had a similar construction: five to eight players, divided into melodic instruments of piano, trumpet, clarinet and trombone and percussion instruments of drums and string bass. All jazz bands have subsequently been organized after this fashion.

SWING Swing music grew directly out of the Dixieland music and was developed in the 1920's and then came to full maturity in the decade of 1935-1945, which is known as the "swing era" and the "big band era." Such names as Duke Ellington, Glenn Miller, Benny Goodman (the King of Swing), Dorsey Brothers and Count Basie are still well known and much of their music is still the basis for swing dancing. The swing bands were large groups, running to fifteen pieces. The Benny Goodman Band played an historic jazz concert in Carnegie Hall in 1938.

BEBOP. This unusual style of music came into being in the 1940's. More for listening than dancing, bebop contains unusual rhythms and strange improvisations. A leader in bebop music was Charlie Parker, saxophonist.

ROCK MUSIC. Also called Rock and Roll, this music came to the fore in the mid-1950's. An outstanding star was Bill Haley and the Comets who produced the recording "Rock Around the Clock'"

Rock music is basically a rhythm-and-blues style but it is characterized by a very hard (solid, powerful) beat. Played in 4/4 meter there are strong accents on the second and fourth beats of the bar. The use of electronic instruments, (electric guitar) also heighten the beat accent.

Rock music contains much singing and nonsense syllables that go off into a chant such as "yeah, yeah, yeah," and "man, oh man, oh man." and endless pleading to "baby, baby, baby." Themes are folk-style, depicting love and affection, the misery of living, the joy of living, the troubles of daily living.

Rock music has bred a succession of dances with names like The Twist, The Monkey, The Frug, The Snake and even Mashed Potatoes. A large part of rock dancing is free style gyrations and contortions as a couple face each other but have no body contact.

Across the centuries of human living, music and dancing have been an integral of life, separately and as a combined behavior. Separately and together they still fill the life of modern man with joy and pleasure.

Chapter 3

The Dance Pattern

To be considered a dance at all, the bodily movements of a person on the dance floor must progress in an orderly manner, in a synchronization with the beat of the music. For example, in the waltz box pattern there will be a step forward, a step to the right, a step backward and then a step to the left, forming a box design. The pattern will then be repeated several times.

All dances--jitterbug, waltz and square dances--are composed of their own peculiar pattern. Indeed, when you set out to "learn to dance" you are really starting to learn a pattern of steps called waltz, swing and tango.

In this book we have collated ten factors that, when taken as a whole, constitute a dance pattern. Other elements might be added for a particular dance but there cannot be less than the ten elements given here.

It should be borne in mind that the basic pattern does not include turns, twists, torso movements or unusual figures. These factors are learned as one gains ability in dancing, either alone or from a dance instructor, while the instruction given here is basic, is the frame-work of the dance and upon which turns and figures are attached.

The ten ingredients that compose the structure of a dance, as shown in Part II, are as follows:

PART A - THE BASIC CONDITION

1. The normal action of the dance, whether slow or fast, smooth or uneven.
2. The position to take at the start of a dance, such as the couple facing each other or aligned side by side as in line dancing.
3. Time signature: 3/4, 2/4 or 4/4 time.
4. The tempo: number of measures per minute.
5. The accent beat, which emphasizes the strong beat of a measure.

PART B - THE STEP PATTERN OF THE DANCE

The pattern is presented in table form of which there are four columns plus a line to show the total count of the pattern. With the step pattern in table format the information can be readily seen and held before the eyes to learn and practice the pattern.

6. Column #1 shows the sequence and direction of the steps.
7. Col. #2 gives the rhythm count and the accented beats, with a right carot.
8. Col. #3 gives the step time, the duration of the step.
9. Col. #4 shows the foot step, the part of the foot that is placed on the floor, such as flat, toe, ball of the foot.
10. The line under the table is the total count contained in the pattern.

The task in dancing is to learn and perform these ten factors as they apply to each dance.

Chapter 4

The Learning Process

Every individual--you, I, our friends-- learn, (gather new information) each in our own way and at a different pace. If this were not so we would all be perfect dancers or perfect dunces. And of course we all fit somewhere in between these extremes--because we each learn at our own particular pace. So we cannot give a mathematical formula for learning because such a scheme has not yet been invented. However, there are certain central points that apply to dance learning and it is these that we shall review in this brief chapter.

1.   As we have shown in Chapter 3, the instruction is given in table form, that is, it presented in a concise manner of columns and rows.   The advantage to this is that all basic information for each dance is concentrated in one place and so there is no need to leaf back and forth in the book for instruction on the waltz or tango because each is shown in one place. Another advantage is that the book may be held in the hand, "seen at a glance" as the dance is being practiced. The information can be absorbed as a unit, that of reading and performing at the same time.

2.   Try and view the first three columns as one unit of action:

(a).   The pattern of steps -- forward, backward, side.

(b).   The rhythm count -- 1, 2, 3; 1, 2, 3.

(c).   Duration of steps -- S, Q, Q; S, Q, Q.

These three elements are the heart of every dance and must be known so that they can be repeated "by heart" as you dance along on the dance floor.

3.   The tables will require long and detailed study, over and over, and then practiced over and over until they "set" in the mind. Some call his learning "muscle memory." which is only partly true.   It is part mind memory and part muscle conditioning.

4.   Do not look upon the tables as being "meager"in information just because they are small in size. Statistical tables are an instrument for transmitting information by condensing it into a small space. Then, too, one can range up and down and across to compare and contrast one entry with another, thus gaining a second and perspective view. So the tables are small but they contain much.

5.   As you are learning, it is helpful to speak the rhythm and step duration out loud. This way you both see and hear the information which is quite helpful in the learning process. For example, suppose the pattern is LF forward, RF forward, LF to the side, RF close to LF. (Foxtrot).

First, count the rhythm a few times: 1, 2, 3, 4; 1, 2, 3, 4.

Then, count the step time (duration) a few times:

S, S, Q , Q;   S, S, Q, Q.

6.   Each dance pattern has a proper beginning, especially with a dance partner, as follows:

•   Go to the edge of the floor, stand side by side, and then enter the floor together.

•   Confront your partner, the man facing the direction of the line of dance (LOD).

•   Stand in the correct position: embraced, closed, apart, etc.

•   Stand in good posture, erect, anticipating.

• Before starting to dance, listen closely to the music and recognize the rhythm and the beat.
• Start to dance: the tango, cha cha, swing, waltz.

The people who teach learning, the professors of education, tell us that we never stop learning as long as we live. And the great teachers of dancing say that this is quite true of dancing--after we become experts in the skill of dancing there will still be much to learn. Now this is not said to discourage but rather to encourage, for one of the joys of dancing is in learning to dance new patterns. There is as much pleasure in achieving a new routine of steps as there is in performing the routine in dancing, once it has been learned. Learning is gaining the skill while dancing is performing the art (exhibiting the skill), and both bring enjoyment.

Chapter 5

Positions, Steps and Turns

These three terms— a position, a step and a turn—when performed on the dance floor make-up the greater part of all dancing movements. Indeed, they are the three ingredients that constitute "a dance." In other words, they are the building blocks with which to construct the house called "a dance." When these blocks are put together with precise technique and rhythm, one is then performing a dance, a series of movements called waltz or swing, tango or cha cha, line or country dance.

It is essential then that these terms be clearly understood before practice is begun. Accordingly, we have included this glossary chapter of these important terms before describing the dance patterns.

BODY POSITIONS

Position refers to the placement or arrangement of the body proper.

CLOSED POSITION

The couple face each other a few inches apart.

The lady stands slightly to the man's right so that each may see over the shoulder of the other.

The man's left hand holds the lady's right hand, both elbows bent so that the hands are about level with the shoulders.

The man's right arm is curved around the lady's back, hand resting just below her left shoulder blade.

The lady's left arm rests on the man's right arm, with her hand on his shoulder.

APART POSITION

The partners are separated at arms length apart. No physical contact, as we see in disco dancing and much Latin dancing.

PROMENADE POSITION

From the closed position the partners open in to a "vee" shape, facing in the same direction. The hands stay in the same place as in the Closed Position, with hips in near contact except that in the Tango promenade the hips are in direct contact.

OPEN PROMENADE POSITION

Similar to promenade position except that the couple are now about 20 inches apart, hips are not near each other. Partners are in a wide "vee, bodies almost in-line.

The man's left hand releases the lady's right hand and swings freely outward, palm down, right arm still around her waist.

The lady's right hand swings freely.

COUNTER PROMENADE POSITION

The opposite of promenade position. The man's right hand holds the lady's left hand, with the man's left hip and the lady's right hip are in near contact, forming a "V"   This is a restricted position.

OPEN COUNTER PROMENADE POSITION

The opposite of open promenade position.   The man's right hand releases the lady's left hand and the free arms are held at shoulder height, with palms down.

RIGHT OUTSIDE POSITION

Similar to the closed position except that the couple are now in-line, with the man's right shoulder adjacent to the lady's right shoulder, and each facing in the opposite direction.

To go into the right outside position, the couple are dancing along in closed position, then each makes a one-eighth turn to the left and the man steps outside to the left and forward beside the lady. The man's right foot is outside the lady's right foot. Hand holds do not change from closed position hold.

LEFT OUTSIDE POSITION

Opposite from the right outside position maneuver.

CUDDLE POSITIONS

1. RIGHT CUDDLE. The lady is at the man's right side, both facing in the same direction, in the line of dance (LOD). The man has his right arm across the lady's shoulders, the lady had her left arm across the man's shoulders The man's left

hand and the lady's right hand are clasped in front of their bodies. As they walk forward together their inner (adjacent) legs advance together and the outer legs advance together.. (The Gay Gordon's dance is an example).

2. LEFT CUDDLE .   Same procedure as above except that the lady is at the man's left side.

BREAK POSITION

The partners are apart, (no body contact) but are still holding hands, such as we see in the cross-over break in the cha cha and during turning steps.

FIFTH POSITION BREAK

Same as the cross-over break.

FALL AWAY POSITION

A couple traveling backward, in promenade position.

CONTRA BODY MOVEMENT.   See TURNS below.

HAND POSITIONS

IN THE WALTZ, FOX TROT, Etc.
The man's left hand and the lady's right hand are clasped, with arms bent to a vertical position at the elbow and hands at shoulder height.   The four fingers of the man's left hand are closed over the back of the lady's hand.   Arms are close to the body but may be extended outward, floor room permitting.

IN THE SWING DANCE.
The man's left arm is held low, (arm nearly rigid),   his

fingers clutching the lady's clinched fingers.

IN LATIN DANCING

The man's thumb is placed in the palm of the lady's right hand, his fingers over the back of the lady's hand.

IN TURNS.

The man's left hand clasps the lady's right hand   lightly, only the fingers touching.   It is a loose contact that allows for the turning action.

INSIDE HANDS JOINED

When the partners are dancing side-by-side,   the two adjacent hands are held, the outside hands are free.

DANCE STEPS

STEPS IN MOTION

• A Step. The transfer of weight from one foot to another.

• A Walk.   This is one step in one beat: forward, or backward, or in place. The count is 1, 2, 3, 4, that is 4 walks, in 4/4 time.

• Chasse'. This is a step to the side, either right or left, and requires two steps to complete it, thus: left foot to the side then close right foot to the left foot;   right foot to the side then close left foot to the right foot. Referred to as left or right chasse'.

• Triple Step. This is three steps taken to two beats of music, forward, backward or to the side.   It is counted in this fashion: 1 a 2, 3 a 4. As in Polka and Cha Cha.

• Step In Place.   Lift the foot and put it back down in the same place.

• Two Step. It is also called the Two Step Dance, the Texas Two Step and sometimes the Quickstep.

In the Two Step the footwork is "step, close, step," and the rhythmic count is Quick, Quick, Slow.

There are many figures in the Two Step such as turns, back-stepping and arm positions such as the pretzel.

In polka, swing and cha cha the torso is held upright while in country-western Two Step the torso is often held in a leaning position, either left, right or forward.

• Rock Step.   This is a transfer of body weight, with two steps in two beats.   For example: a forward rock step means that a foot is stepped forward (left foot), and weight put on the foot, in beat one, then the body rocks back and weight is placed on the right foot, on beat two. (Thus in the Cha Cha—cha cha cha forward, rock step, cha cha cha backward, rock step).. .

• Vine and Cross Steps.   These steps are similar and are danced either right or left, the exception being that in vining the one foot goes behind the other and in crossing one foot goes in front of the other.   Example:

1. Vine to right: step right foot to the side, cross left foot behind the right foot, step right foot to the side, close left foot to the right foot. (4 counts).

2. Vine to left: step LF to side, cross RF behind LF, step LF to the side, close RF to LF.

Use the same pattern to do cross steps except that one foot crosses in front of instead of behind the other.

• Row Step.   Partners are facing each other, holding hands, then alternate retreating from and approaching each other, with arms extending and returning in a butterfly action.

STEPS IN TIME

• Quick Step. The time duration of a quick step occupies one beat of music. Remember that Quick does not mean Fast.

• Slow Step. The time duration of a slow step occupies two beats of music.

• Double Quick Step. This occupies one-half beat of music. Called the "and" or "a" beat, as in the triple step:

DANCE TURNS

BODY MOVEMENT IN TURNS

Before we define the dance turns themselves we need to describe a certain body motion that precedes the actual turning process itself.

The body movement is a twist of the torso in the direction of the turn. If you are making a left turn, twist the body to the left at the same time the step is being taken or even a split moment before the step.   The same action is taken when turning to the right, twist the torso to the right.

Most authors use the term "Contra Body Movement" but this is a gross error. Just because the right shoulder and right hip turn to the left is not a "contra" movement. The hip and shoulder are part of the torso and so if the torso turns left,the right shoulder and right hip must go along with the torso.

The turn is made in this fashion, (assume a left turn):
1. A 90 or 180 degree left turn:
    a. Extend the left foot forward and twist torso to left.
    b. On ball of left foot, pivot 90 or 180 degrees.

2. A 360 degree turn (and 4/4 time):
    a. Extend the left foot forward and twist the torso left.
    b. Pivot 180 degrees on ball of left foot.
    c. Bring right foot beside left foot and pivot another 180 degrees on the ball of the right foot.

EXTENT OF TURN

Turns are described by the extent of the turn and by the direction, either right or left.
1. Full turn - 360 degrees, left or right.
2. Half turn:- 180 degrees, left or right.
3. Quarter turn - 90 degrees, left or right.
4. One Eight turn - 45 degrees, left or right.

RIGHT TURN, LEFT TURN

For both partners, a right turn is clockwise, a left turn is counter-clockwise.

ARCH TURN

This is a full turn left for the man and a full turn right for the lady. The arch is formed by the raised left hand of the man and the raised right hand of the lady, holding each others hands high to form an arch.   Either party may pass through the arch and make their turn.

LOOP TURN

Similar to the arch turn, it is a full turn right for the man and a full turn left for the lady. The arch is formed by the raised right arm of the man and the raised left arm of the lady. However, the hands are held over the head, not to the side as in the arch turn.

SOLO TURN

The partners have no body contact, only the hands. Hands are lowered to waist level, then released with a flick by the man, in the direction of the turn to be made.

PIVOT TURN

A dancing movement in which the dancer swivels on the ball of one foot while the other foot is placed (stepped) in front of or behind the stationary foot.

TWIST TURN

Done on the heel and toe jointly (flat foot).

SPIN TURN

A turn done in place, on ball of the foot.

* * * * *

NOTE: The times and tempos given in most of the dances desbribed in Part II, (in the tables), are derived from the specifications of the National Dance Council of America.

Chapter 6

Categories of Dancing

There is no standard classification of dances largely because there is much over-lapping in dance figures.   This means that many given dances are performed under two headings.   For example, the polka is a German folk dance and very much a modern ballroom dance; the waltz is historical, a folk dance and a modern, popular dance.   Therefore the following groupings are not exact, rather they designate a normal distinction as the dances are commonly spoken of.   The classifications are Historical Dance, Folk, Modern, National and Theater Dances.

The term "jazz dance" is frequently used but this is inaccurate.   People do not jazz dance, they dance to jazz music, though some stage actors are billed as "jazz dancers."

The term "social dance" is a catch-all for everything and has no meaning as a dance pattern.   All dancing is social in nature as it refers to a group of persons in social behavior. Just two persons together is a social condition so if Robinson Crusoe had had a dancing partner on his island it would have been a social dance.

Probably the use of the term "social dancing" would be accurately applied to the kingly courts of Europe where partner dancing began.   The minuet first appeared in the French court of Louis XIV around 1650 and was widely danced thereafter.

HISTORICAL DANCES

'Historical' is a loose term that applies to the early partner dancing. Some examples are the allemande, bourree, cotillion, courante,   gavotte,   minuet,   pavane,   quadrille,   rigadoon, schottische, volta.

FOLK DANCES

These are dances that have an ethnic quality to them, are traditional dances of a class of people. Some examples are: Highland Fling, eightsome reel,   the jig, hornpipe, morris dancing, square dance, sword dance (Scottish).   (See also the National Dances below).

MODERN-POPULAR DANCES

The following group of dances are the dances of today, the dancing of *The People* in the ballroom and dance halls across the country. Again, exactness is difficult because   of improvisation as we see in the swing which has three versions: single swing, double swing and triple swing.   It is further complicated by an Eastern Swing and a Western Swing.

BALLROOM and LATIN DANCING

Strict ballroom: Waltz, Foxtrot, swing, polka, quickstep, Gay Gordons
Combined Ballroom and Latin: Cha Cha, Rumba, Tango.

LINE DANCING

Of recent vintage, the Line Dance is very popular.   The dancers are arranged in a line, side by side, and perform intricate steps to the beat of music.   Line dancers do not have partners as in Ballroom and Latin dances.

Some dance titles are: the Electric Slide, Tush Push, Cotton Eyed   Joe, Honky Tonk Stomp.,   Boot Scootin' Boogie, Slapping' Leather, Cowboy Cha Cha.

COUNTRY SQUARE DANCING

This is partner dancing in which the partners, eight persons, form a square, facing each other, for a starting position.   This position soon breaks up into intricate patterns although the square is kept intact.

These dances are "called", that is, a person calls out the pattern to perform and the dancers "step to the tune of the caller."

A dance is a "set" with such titles as Birdie in the Cage, Shoot the Owl, Texas Star, Wagon Wheel, Red River Valley and Grapeville Twist.

Music includes: Alabama Girl, Camptown Races, Devil's Dream, Shoo Fly, Turkey in the Straw, Virginia Reel.

COUNTRY AND WESTERN DANCING

This class of dancing has several titles: Country Dancing, Kicker Dancing (in Texas), Western Dancing, Cowboy Dancing.

Country and Western is danced largly as a couple dance but also with couples linked together in a line position. Dancing is lively with a fast tempo.

Cowboy duds are usually worn: hat, boots and fancy shirt, both by the man and the woman.

DISCO (Discotheque) DANCING

Disco is danced either with a partner or solo. Some titles are: Basic Hustle, Latin Hustle, Tango Hustle, Disco Swing, N.Y. Huastle. Line Hustle, Twist.

LATINO DANCES

These are Salsa Dances. Salsa is Spanish for sauce and the dances are indeed saucy.

The various types of dances are: Merengue, Samba, Mambo (cumbia),   Salsa, Paso Doble,   Fast Rumba (with Box step, butterfly, Cuban back rock, cross over break, Bolero, plena), Mozambique.

SOME NATIONAL DANCES

Spanish - bolero, fandago, flamenco, zapateado, seguidilla.
Brazilian - bossa nova, maxixe.
French - farandole, tambourin.
German - galop.
Cuban - habanera.
Isralli - hora.
Maori - haka.
Polunesian - hula.
Russian - kazatzka.
Caribbean - limbo.
Polish - polonaise, mazurka.
Italian - saltarello, tarantella

THEATRICAL DANCING

These are dances performed by trained, professional persons to entertain the public.   Such dancing requires high skill, disciplined training, years of practice and stylistic movements.

The dances have a realistic meaning as they depict tragedy and comedy, joy of life, sorrow and happiness. Costumes are used. Dances include ballet, dramatic exhibition, theatrical performance.

PART II

PATTERNS OF THE DANCE

* * *

In this section we shall present the patterns that form the structure of a dance.   We shall describe the basic steps only of the several classes of dancing known as Ballroom, Latin. Country and Western, Line, Disco and Latino Dances.

We cannot, of course, define every pattern of these dances, only the basic steps and beat because, to delineate every pattern would require an encyclopedia.   However, the difficult part of learning to dance is to learn the basic pattern.   When this is known then the other patterns of that dance are merely a variation of the basic pattern and can be learned with ease.

In Chapter 3, *The Dance Pattern,* we enumerated the ten prime points of a dance structure and these points might be reviewed at this time, to one's advantage.

ABBREVIATIONS FREQUENTLY USED

To conserve space and expedite the learning process we have employed a group of abbreviations that are frequently used in the descriptions.   The abbreviations are in common use in the dance community.

LF - Left foot.

RF - Right foot.

Q - Quick step. (Equals one beat of music).

S - Slow step. (Equals two beats of music and of course

equals two quick steps).

PP - Promenade position.

CPP - Counter promenade position.

LOD - Line of dance (counter-clockwise around the floor).

CW - Clockwise around the dance floor.

CCW - Counter clockwise around the dance floor.

Additional - Foot means a step with weight of the body on the foot. (Toe, heel, rock and brush steps do not have body weight on the foot. In these, one leg is merely extended outward while the other leg sustains the body weight.)

Chapter 7

The Waltz

The waltz was first danced as a country folk dance in Germany in a clumsy fashion and then stylized for the ballroom, for "gentle folk" dancing. The waltz was very popular in Europe in the mid-1800's when Johann Strauss composed his beautiful music.

This is a smooth, even dance, characterized by a wave-like motion of rise-and-fall of the body plus frequent turns. It is also of simple structure and therefore an ideal dance to start with when you begin the process of learning the skill of dancing. The waltz is popular throughout the world and if there is such a thing as an international dance, it is the waltz.

There are two versions of the waltz. First is the American/English style which is danced at a tempo of 30 to 40 measures per minute. Secondly, the Viennese style is danced at 50 to 60 measures per minute thus requiring a much faster stepping pace than the American/English waltz. We will define the American/English waltz here.

As we shall do in every dance description, we will describe the basic pattern of the dance, being in this case the Progressive Forward pattern of the waltz.   We have included also the Box figure and the quarter turns.

STRUCTURE OF THE WALTZ

PART A - BASIC CONDITIONS

THE NORMAN ACTION. The waltz is an even-paced dance, unlike such dances as the jitterbug and the disco.   It is danced progressively around the LOD and also danced in a close space, as in the box pattern.

POSITION AT THE START. This is a partner dance entirely, danced in the closed position.   Begin with feet together, posture erect.

TIME SIGNATURE. 3/4 Time.

TEMPO: 30 bars per minute.

ACCENT: Rhythm Count one. (see carot mark).

PART B - PATTERN OF THE WALTZ

READING DOWN EACH COLUMN:
  Col. 1 - Practice the steps without music.
  Col. 2 - With music playing, put rhythm to the steps.
  Col. 3 - Put duration of time to the steps.
  Col. 4 - Put foot position to the steps.

PROGRESSIVE WALTZ FIGURE - For the Man

Pattern of the Steps	Rhythm Count	Step Time	Type Step
LF Forward	1>	Slow	Flat
RF Forward	2	Quick	Ball
LF Forward	3	Quick	Ball
RF Forward	1>	Slow	Flat
LF Forward	2	Quick	Ball
RF Forward	3	Quick	Ball

Total Count: 1, 2, 3;   4, 5, 6.

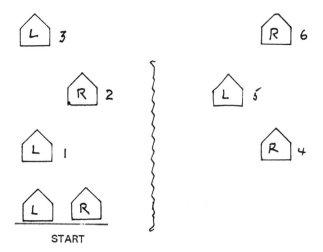

START

PROGRESSIVE WALTZ FIGURE - For the Lady

Pattern of the Steps	Rhythm Count	Step Time	Type Step
RF Backward	1>	Slow	Flat
LF Backward	2	Quick	Ball
RF Backward	3	Quick	Ball
LF Backward	1>	Slow	Flat
RF Backward	2	Quick	Ball
LF Backward	3	Quick	Ball

Total Count: 1, 2, 3;   4, 5, 6.

WALTZ BOX FIGURE - For the Man

Pattern of the Steps	Rhythm Count	Step Time	Type Step
LF Forward	1>	Slow	Flat
RF to Side	2	Quick	Ball
LF Close RF	3	Quick	Ball
RF Backward	1>	Slow	Flat
LF to Side	2	Quick	Ball
RF Close LF	3	Quick	Ball

Total Count: 1, 2, 3; 4, 5, 6.

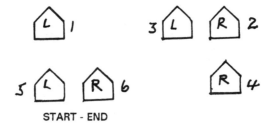

START - END

WALTZ BOX FIGURE - For the Lady

Pattern of the Steps	Rhythm Count	Step Time	Type Step
RF Backward	1>	Slow	Flat
LF to Side	2	Quick	Ball
RF Close LF	3	Quick	Ball
LF Forward	1>	Slow	Flat
RF to Side	2	Quick	Ball
LF Close RF	3	Quick	Ball

Total Count: 1, 2, 3;   4, 5, 6.

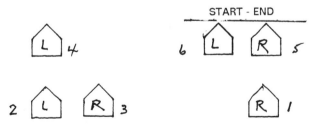

THE WALTZ QUARTER TURNS

The description below is for the Waltz Quarter Turns, left and right - for the man.

The lady's steps will be the opposite of the man's.

Use the Box Figure - For the man.

Make the turns on counts 2, 5, 8, and 11.

1 - Left foot forward.
2 - Right foot to side (make 1/4 turn to the right).
3 - Left foot closed right foot.

4 - Right foot back.
5 - Left foot to the side (make quarter turn to the right)..
6 - Right foot close left foot.

7 - Left foot back.
8 - Right foot to side (make quarter turn to left).
9 - Left foot close right foot.

10 - Right foot forward.
11 - Left foot to side (make quarter turn to left).]
12 - Right foot close left foot.

ADDITIONAL WALTZ FIGURES

Half box progressive.   Half box turn.
Cross step.   Outside position (twinkle).
Left and right quarter turns (given above).

Chapter 8

The Foxtrot

The name "foxtrot" does not refer to the pace of that wily animal the fox, rather it is a dance introduced by Harry Fox, a New York choreographer, about 1912.

The foxtrot is danced at a moderate pace, to modern type music, by a couple. We shall present the Foxtrot Progressive Figure and the Box Figure

STRUCTURE OF THE FOX TROT

PART A - BASIC CONDITIONS

THE NORMAL ACTION: A moderate walking action, even paced, smooth. with arm movements that lend elegance.

POSITION AT THE START: Danced in closed position. Couple face each other, erect posture, torso stationary, weight on balls of feet.

TIME SIGNATURE: 4/4 time.

TEMPO: 32 Measures Per Minute.

PART B - PATTERN OF THE DANCE

READING DOWN EACH COLUMN :
   Col. 1 - Practice the steps without music.
   Col 2 - With music playing, put rhythm to the steps.
   Col. 3 - Add duration of time to the steps.
   Col. 4 - Add foot position to the steps.

PROGRESSIVE FOXTROT - For the Man

Pattern of the Steps	Rhythm Count	Step Time	Type Step
LF Forward	1 &	Slow	Flat
RF Forward	2 & >	Slow	Flat
LF to Side	3	Quick	Flat
RF close LF	4 >	Quick	Flat

Total count: 1- 2,   3 - 4,   5,   6.

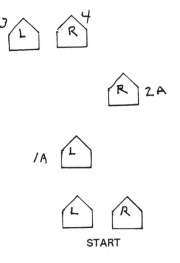

START

PROGRESSIVE FOXTROT - For the Lady

Pattern of the Steps	Rhythm Count	Step Time	Type Step
RF Backward	1 &	Slow	Flat
LF Backward	2 & >	Slow	Flat
RF to Side	3	Quick	Flat
LF close RF	4 >	Quick	Flat

Total count: 1 - 2, 3 - 4, 5, 6.

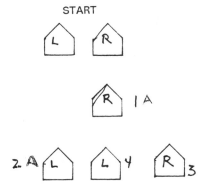

FOXTROT BOX FIGURE - For the Man

Pattern of the Steps	Rhythm Count	Step Time	Type Step
LF Forward	1	Quick	Flat
RF close LF	2 >	Quick	Toe
RF to Side	3	Quick	Flat
LF close RF	4 >	Quick	Ftat
RF Backward	1	Quick	Flat
LF close RF	2 >	Quick	Toe
LF to Side	3	Quick	Flat
RF close LF	4 >	Quick	Flat

Total count: 1, 2, 3, 4;   5, 6, 7, 8.

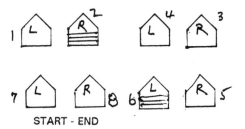

START - END

FOXTROT BOX FIGURE - For the Lady

Pattern of the Steps	Rhythm Count	Step Time	Type Step
RF Backward	1	Quick	Flat
LF Close RF	2 >	Quick	Toe
LF to Side	3	Quick	Flat
RF close LF	4 >	Quick	Flat
LF Forward	1	Quick	Flat
RF Close LF	2 >	Quick	Toe
RF to Side	3	Quick	Flat
LF close RF	4 >	Quick	Flat

Total count: 1, 2, 3, 4,   5, 6, 7, 8.

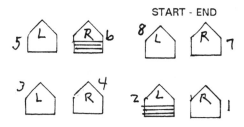

Chapter 9

The Single Swing
(EASTERN STYLE)

Swing music can be traced back to the olden days of Negro Folk music of the South but its immediate ancestor was ragtime music played in New Orleans, the Dixieland style of music of the 1920's. It flourished during the decade of 1935-45 when the Big Bands played and it is still a foremost style today, in both music and dancing. It is "swing" because it has a smoother flow than ragtime.

There are two types of swing dancing that are the most popular, the single count and the triple count. We shall review these in that order in this and the following chapter. We should note that the dance also goes by the name of Lindy, (after Charles Lindbergh, who flew across the Atlantic Ocean non-stop from New York to Paris in 1927) the Jive and the Jitterbug.

The steps in the single swing are almost identical to those of the triple swing, but two differences are to be noted:
1. In the single swing the count is 1-2, 3-4, 5, 6. In the triple swing the count is 1-a-2, 3-a-4, 5, 6.
2. In single swing the steps are unequal because the time is altered in the steps by a hold (pause). In triple swing the steps are unequal because they combine two step movements: a triple step and a one step.

The single Lindy and the Shag have a similar rhythm count and step duration of : slow-slow-quick-quick.

Some swing figures in addition to those given below are:

Underarm turns	Back-to-back turn
Sweetheart wrap	Butterfly
Kick	Pivot turn
Twist	Arm Slide

STRUCTURE OF THE SINGLE SWING

PART A - BASIC CONDITIONS

THE NORMAL ACTION. The nicknames for the swing -- the Lindy hop and the jitterbug dance -- describe the action: a varied stepping and body movement with much improvising of body turns and arm actions, as the dance progresses.

POSITION AT THE START. The posture is upright, feet together. The man's left arm is held downward, holding the lady's right hand in a clutch position. The man's right arm is curved around the lady's body with hand below the shoulder blade, the lady's left arm resting on the man's shoulder.

TIME SIGNATURE: 4/4 time.

TEMPO: Average 44 measures per minute.

ACCENT: On counts 2 and 4.

PART B - PATTERN OF THE DANCE

READING DOWN EACH COLUMN:
Col. 1: Practice the steps without music.
Col. 2: With music playing, put rhythm to the steps.
Col. 3: Put duration of time to the steps.
Col. 4: Put foot position to the steps.

SINGLE SWING - Pattern for the Man

Pattern of the Steps	Rhythm Count	Step Time	Type Step
LF to the Side	1	Slow	Flat
RF touch LF	&		Toe
RF to the Side	2	Slow	Flat
LF touch RF	&		Toe
LF Backward	3	Quick	Ball
RF step In Place	4	Quick	Flat

Total count: 1, 2, 3, 4, 5, 6.

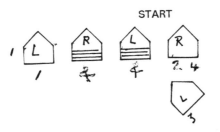

SINGLE SWING - Pattern for the Lady

Pattern of the Steps	Rhythm Count	Step Time	Type Step
RF to the Side	1	Slow	Flat
LF touch RF	&		Toe
LF to the Side	2	Slow	Flat
RF touch LF	&		Toe
RF Backward	3	Quick	Ball
LF step In Place	4	Quick	Flat

Total count: 1, 2, 3, 4, 5, 6.

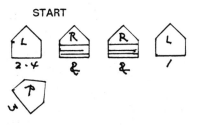

Chapter 10

The Triple Swing
(EASTERN STYLE)

This version of the swing dance is nearly identical to the single swing except for the following:

1. The rhythmic count in single swing is: 1-2, 3-4, 5, 6. The count in triple swing is: 1-a-2, 3-a-4, 5, 6.

2, The tempo is fast in the single swing (44 BPM) and slow in triple swing (40 BPM), thus allowing for the extra rhythm step.

STRUCTURE OF THE TRIPLE SWING

PART A - BASIC CONDITIONS

THE NORMAL ACTION. Very active with turns, arm movements, improvising.

POSITION AT START. Partner's face each other, posture upright and feet together, man's left arm downward holding the lady's right hand, torso erect but may lean to left and right during the dance.

TIME SIGNATURE: 4/4 time.

TEMPO: 40 measures per minute.

ACCENT: On 2nd and 4th beat.

PART B - PATTERN OF THE DANCE

READING DOWN EACH COLUMN:
  Col. 1: Practice the steps without music.
  Col. 2: With music playing, put rhythm to the steps.
  Col. 3: Put duration of time to the steps.
  Col. 4: Put foot position to the steps.

TRIPLE SWING - Pattern for the Man

Pattern of the Steps	Rhythm Count	Step Time	Type Step
Triple Step Left:			
LF step Left	1	Quick	Flat
RF close LF	&	Quick	Ball
LF step In Place	2 >	Slow	Flat
Triple Step Right:			
RF step Right	3	Quick	Flat
LF close RF	&	Quick	Ball
RF step in Place	4 >	Slow	Flat
LF Back	5	Quick	Ball
RF step in Place	6 >	Quick	Change

Total count: 1, 2, 3, 4, 5, 6, 7, 8.

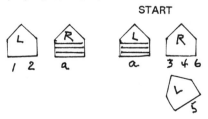

TRIPLE SWING - Pattern for the Lady

Pattern of the Steps	Rhythm Count	Step Time	Type Step
Triple Step Right:			
RF to Side	1	Quick	Flat
LF close RF	&	Quick	Ball
RF step in Place	2 >	Slow	Flat
Triple Step Left:			
LF to the side	3	Quick	Flat
RF close LF	&	Quick	Ball
LF step in Place	4 >	Slow	Flat
RF step back	5	Quick	Ball
LF step in Place	6 >	Quick	Change

Total count: 1, 2, 3, 4, 5, 6., 7, 8.

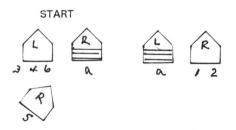

The Polka

The Polka is a German folk dance and has changed remarkably little over the years although there are modern trimmings.   Much of the early dancing was done by couples aligned side-by-side while most polka dancing today is by a couple facing each other.

The proper step of the Polka begins with a hop, on the upbeat count. The rhythmic count, starting on the upbeat is: &-1, &-2, &-3, &-4.

But most ballroom Polka of today begins with a triple step, starting on the downbeat, thus eliminating the upbeat hop. The triple step is really a modified hop.

STRUCTURE OF THE POLKA

PART A - BASIC CONDITIONS

THE NORMAL ACTION.   There are three types of Polka commonly danced today, as follows.

1. A couple dancing in close space.   This is two persons embraced in the closed position, facing each other,   who dance the polka in a confined area, turning as they dance.

2. A couple dancing a progressive Polka. In this case the couple stand side-by-side, man on the lady's left, with adjacent arms interlocked at the elbow and outside hands on their hips. They circle the floor in a constant forward movement in a CCW direction.

3.   A group dancing a progressive Polka. This is a group of persons, couples or individuals, aligned side-by-side, facing the LOD, arms around each others shoulders, and dancing forward around the dance floor in a CCW direction.

POSITION AT THE START   (For couple in close area). Partners face each other in the Closed Position.

TIME SIGNATURE: 2/4.

TEMPO: 44 measures per minute.

ACCENT: Counts 1 and 3.

PART B - PATTERN OF THE DANCE

READING DOWN EACH COLUMN:
Col. 1 - Practice the steps without music.
Col. 2 - With music playing, put rhythm to the steps.
Col. 3 - Now add duration of time to the steps.
Col. 4 - Then add foot position to the steps.

COUPLE POLKA - Pattern for the Man

Pattern of the Steps	Rhythm Count	Step Time	Type Step
First Half			
Step LF in place	1>	Quick	Flat
Step RF in place	a	Quick	Ball
Step LF in place	2	Slow	Flat
Second Half			
Step RF in place	3>	Quick	Flat
Step LF in place	a	Quick	Ball
Step RF in place	4	Slow	Flat

Total count: 1, 2, 3, 4, 5, 6, 7, 8.

The pattern of steps given above means to "step in place" in a circling movement.

START

COUPLE POLKA - Pattern for the Lady

Pattern of the Steps	Rhythm Count	Step Time	Type Step
First Half:			
Step RF in place	1>	Quick	Flat
Step LF in place	a	Quick	Ball
Step RF in place	2	Slow	Flat
Second Half:			
Step LF in place	3>	Quick	Flat
Step RF in place	a	Quick	Ball
Step LF in place	4	Slow	Flat

Total count: 1, 2, 3, 4, 5, 6, 7, 8.

The pattern of steps given above means to "step in place" in a circling movement.

PROGRESSIVE POLKA - Pattern for a group.

Pattern of the Steps	Rhythm Count	Step Type	Type Step
Do 4 triple steps:			
L - R - L	1-a-2	Quick	F-toe-F
R - L - R	3-a-4	Quick	F-toe-F
L - R - L	5-a-6	Quick	F-toe-F
R - L - R	7-a-8	Quick	F-toe-F
LF Forward	1	Quick	Heel
LF close RF	2	Quick	Flat
RF Backward	3	Quick	Toe
RF close LF	4	Quick	Flat
RF Forward	5	Quick	Heel
RF close LF	6	Quick	Flat
LF kick across RF	7	Quick	Heel
LF close RF	8	Quick	Kick
Repeat triple steps			

Total count: 1, 2, 3, 4, 5, 6, 7, 8.

Chapter 12

The Rumba

The Rumba is often regarded to be the classic dance of all of the Latin dances. It came to the U. S. about 1930 and has remained a very popular dance ever since.

The Rumba is identified with Cuba and the famous Cuban Hip Movement and the strong accent on beats 1 and 4. The steps in the Rumba are simple and it is generally considered to a dance that is easy to learn and to perform.

The Rumba contains many figures including:

Under arm turn	Progressive forward
5th position break	Cross body step
Right back turn	Walk around
Butterfly break	Wheel turn

We shall show below the Box Pattern, the basic one.

STRUCTURE OF THE RUMBA

PART A - BASIC CONDITIONS

THE NORMAL ACTION.: A moderate rhythm with accented hip movements.

POSITION AT THE START: Danced in closed position.

TIME SIGNATURE: 4/4.

TEMPO: 27 to 30 bars per minute.

ACCENT: Counts 1 and 4.

PART B - PATTERN OF THE DANCE

READING DOWN EACH COLUMN:
Col. 1: Practice the steps without music.
Col. 2: With music playing, put rhythm to the steps.
Col. 3: Put duration of time to the steps.
Col. 4: Put foot position to the steps.

THE RUMBA - Pattern for the Man

Pattern of the Steps	Rhythm Count	Step Time	Type Step
LF Forward	1 >	Quick	Flat
RF to side	2	Quick	Flat
LF close RF	3	Slow	Flat
RF Backward	4 >	Quick	Flat
LF to side	5	Quick	Flat
RF close LF	6	Slow	Flat

Total count: 1, 2, 3, 4, 5, 6.

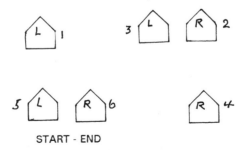

START - END

THE RUMBA - Pattern for the Lady

Pattern of the Steps	Rhythm Count	Step Time	Type Step
RF Backward	1 >	Quick	Flat
LF to side	2	Quick	Flat
RF close L	3	Slow	Flat
LF Forward	4 >	Quick	Flat
RF to side	5	Quick	Flat
LF close RF	6	Slow	Flat

Total count: 1, 2, 3, 4, 5, 6.

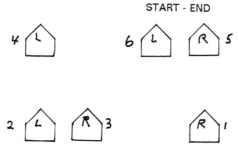

START - END

Chapter 13

The Cha Cha

The Cha Cha is one of the most popular of all Latin dances. It is made-up of triple steps, cross-overs and rock steps and resembles somewhat the American Swing. (In British dancing the triple steps are called "three linked steps, a good descriptive term).

The Cha Cha is usually assigned to Cuba as its origin but it does contain elements of several Latino dances, especially the Rumba.

STRUCTURE OF THE CHA CHA

PART A - BASIC CONDITIONS

THE NORMAL ACTION. The Cha Cha is danced in two versions:
1. The American version is danced with a rocking motion.
2. The Cuban version is danced with the Cuban hip movement emphasized, that is, the alternate lifting and bending of the knees which causes the hips to protrude.

Ordinarily, on the dance floor, both versions are employed.

POSITION AT THE START. This is a couple dance with the partners facing each other in the closed position.

TIME SIGNATURE. 4/4 time.

TEMPO.   32 measures per minute.

ACCENT.   First beat of the measure.

STARTING TO DANCE THE CHA CHA

In much of the Latin music there is a "tricky" eighth note just prior to the beginning measure. (Or, the last note of the introductory measure). Now it is possible to dance the Cha Cha, from beginning to end, ignoring this eighth note but the dancing will not be in exact time with the music. This note must be taken into account if you are to dance the Cha Cha with the exact beat of the music.

To account for this eighth note one must take an "entering," a "lead-in" step at the beginning. (In British dancing it is called a "preparatory step"). When this step is taken as an entering step, then the Cha Cha will be danced in exact time with the music, and danced with more pleasure.

In the pattern description below we have used an X as the rhythmic count number. But remember—this step is only performed once and that is when entering the cha cha pattern. Remember also that if you stop in the middle of the dance you should "re-enter" with the X step.

PART B - PATTERN OF THE DANCE

READING DOWN EACH COLUMN:
    Col. 1: Practice the steps, by walking, without music.
    Col. 2: With music playing, put rhythm to the steps.
    Col. 3: Put duration of time to the steps.
    Col. 4: Put foot position to the steps.

The CHA CHA - Pattern for the Man

Pattern of the Steps		Rhythm Count	Step Time	Type Step
Entering- Step LF to side		X	Quick	Flat
RF backward	rock-	1	Slow	Ball
LF forward	step	2	Slow	Flat
RF forward	cha-	3	Quick	Flat
LF forward	cha-	&	Quick	Flat
RF forward	cha	4	Slow	Flat
LF forward	rock-	5	Slow	Ball
RF backward	step	6	Slow	Flat
LF backward	cha-	7	Quick	Flat
RF backward	cha-	&	Quick	Flat
LF backward	cha	8	Slow	Flat

Total count: 1, 2, 3 & 4; 5, 6, 7 & 8.

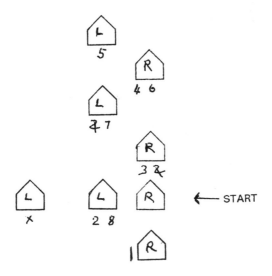

The CHA CHA - Pattern for the Lady

Pattern of the Steps		Rhythm Count	Step Time	Type Step
Entering - Step RF to side		X	Quick	Flat
LF forward	rock-	1	Slow	Ball
RF backward	step	2	Slow	Flat
LF backward	cha-	3	Quick	Flat
RF backward	cha-	&	Quick	Flat
LF backward	cha	4	Slow	Flat
RF backward	rock-	5	Slow	Ball
LF forward	step	6	Slow	Flat
RF forward	cha-	7	Quick	Flat
LF forward	cha-	&	Quick	Flat
RF forward	cha	8	Slow	Flat

Total count: 1, 2, 3 & 4; 5, 6, 7 & 8.

Chapter 14

The Tango

The Tango originated in Argentina a hundred years ago and was danced in the streets and saloons by the poor people. Strong erotic motions were used in the dance and when first introduced into America and England it was considered too immodest to be danced in ballrooms. It was strictly forbidden in some states of the U.S. But as time passed the Tango was modified for dancing in polite company.

STRUCTURE OF THE TANGO

PART A - BASIC CONDITIONS

THE NORMAL ACTION. The Tango is a dramatic dance with rigid, erect posture; clean, sharp steps; and smart head turns to look at your partner and to look in the direction in which you (the couple) are proceeding (forward or to the side).

The dancing always begins on the downbeat, the first beat of the measure.

POSITION AT START. This is very much a couple dance and is danced in the closed position.

TIME SIGNATURE. 4/4 time. (2/4 split). (Use 8 count).

TEMPO. 33 bars per minute.

ACCENT May accent all.

PART B - PATTERN OF THE DANCE

READING DOWN EACH COLUMN:
   Col. 1: Practice the steps by walking, without music.
   Col..2: With music playing, put rhythm to the steps.
   Col. 3: Put duration of time to the steps.
   Col. 4: Put foot position to the steps.

THE TANGO - Pattern for the Man
(Basic Pattern)

Pattern of the Steps	Rhythm Count	Step Time	Type Step
LF forward	1 - 2	Slow	Flat
RF forward	3 - 4	Slow	Flat
LF forward	5	Quick	Flat
RF diagonal forward	6	Quick	Ball
LF close RF	7 - 8	Slow	Flat

Total count: 1, 2, 3, 4, 5, 6, 7, 8.

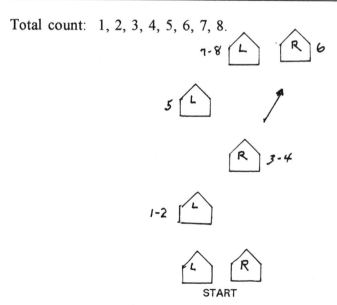

THE TANGO - Pattern for the Lady
(Basic Pattern)

Pattern of the Steps	Rhythm Count	Stwep Time	Type Step
RF backward	1 - 2	Slow	Flat
LF backward	3 - 4	Slow	Flat
RF backward	5	Quick	Flat
LF diagonal backward	6	Quick	Ball
RF close LF	7 - 8	Slow	Flat

Total count: 1, 2, 3, 4, 5, 6, 7, 8.

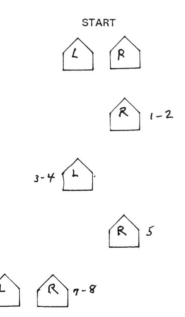

SOME ADDITIONAL FIGURES:
Promenade, Corte', Outer Fan, Inner Fan, Ronde.

Chapter 15

The Merengue

The Merengue is a Latino dance that originated in the Caribbean and came to the United States about 1940. Both Haiti and the Dominican Republic claim to be the source of origin. The Merengue is written in 2/4 time (cut) and danced in 4/4 time. The step pattern is quite simple and generally regarded to be an easy dance to learn. As in most Larin dances the hips play a prominent part while the whole body expresses the rhythm of the music.

STRUCTURE OF THE MERENGUE

PART A -BASIC CONDITIONS

THE NORMAL ACTION. In the basic action the man dips his body on the even counts and the lady dips on the odd counts. This dipping and straightening creates a rocking image of the dancing couple. An alternate to the dipping/bending is the use of the Cuban hip movement, used liberally thoughout the dance. Most steps are on the flat of the foot to accentuate the hip motion.

POSITION AT THE START.   Partners face each other and   dance in the closed position, or else dance in the   apart position, or else the two positions may be changed as the dance proceeds.

TIME SIGNATURE.   4/4 time.

TEMPO.   50 bars per minute.

PART B - PATTERN OF THE DANCE

READING DOWN EACH COLUMN:
   Col. 1: Practice the steps, by walking, without music.
   Col. 2:   With music playing, put rhythm to the steps.
   Col. 3: Add duration of time to the steps.
   Col. 4: Add foot position to the steps.

Figures sketched are the Forward-Backward Walk and the Chasse'. Some additional figures are: Under arm turn, Throw out, Cross Step, Twist.

THE BASIC MERENGUE - Dominican Walk
Pattern for the Man

Pattern of the Steps	Rhythm Count	Step Time	Type Step
LF forward	1	Quick	Flat
RF close to LF	2	Quick	Ball
LF slide step foreward	3 - &	Slow	Flat
RF backward	1	Quick	Flat
LF close to RF	2	Quick	Ball
RF slide step backward	3 - &	Slow	Flat

Total count: 1, 2, 3, 4,   5, 6, 7, 8.

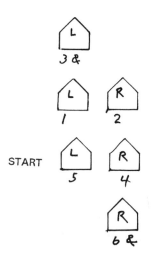

BASIC MERENGUE - Dominican Walk
Pattern for the Lady

Pattern of the Steps	Rhythm Count	Step Time	Type Step
RF backward	1	Quick	Flat
LF close to RF	2	Quick	Ball
RF slide step backward	3 - &	Slow	Flat
LF forward	1	Quick	Flat
RF close to LF	2	Quick	Ball
LF slide step forward	3 - &	Slow	Flat

Total count: 1, 2, 3, 4,   5, 6, 7, 8.

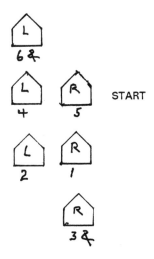

THE MERENGUE - CHASSE'

May be danced in the closed, promenade or apart positions.

Pattern for the Man

Pattern of the Steps	Rhythm Count	Step Time	Type Step
LF to the side	1	Quick	Flat
Slide RF to LF	2	Quick	Ball
LF to the side	3- &	Slow	Flat
RF to the side	1	Quick	Flat
Slide LF to the RF	2	Quick	Ball
RF to the side	3 - &	Slow	Flat

Total count: 1, 2, 3, 4,   5, 6, 7, 8.

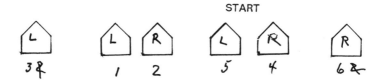

START

MERENGUE CHASSE'

Pattern for the Lady

Pattern for the Lady	Rhythm Count	Step Time	Type Step
RF to the side	1	Quick	Flat
Slide LF to RF	2	Quick	Ball
RF to the side	3- &	Slow	Flat
LF to the side	1	Quick	Flat
Slide RF to LF	2	Quick	Ball
LF to the side	3 - &	Slow	Flat

Total count: 1, 2, 3, 4,   5, 6, 7, 8.

START

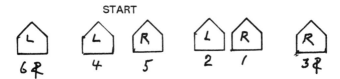

Chapter 16

The Mambo

The Mambo is a Latin (Latino) dance that originated in Haiti and entered the Western culture about 1950. The word "Mambo" is reported to be that of a voodoo priestess in African religion and was carried to Haiti by Negro slaves.

The Mambo is an off-beat dance that has a jagged rhythm in which the dance step is not accented at the same time that the musical note is accented.

The Mambo is often called the "dancing on two dance" because the dancing starts on the second beat of the measure, not on the first beat. In other word you take no steps on counts 1 and 5, you "hold" these steps. Some instructors allow a toe tap instead of a hold.

In the table below is shown the basic Mambo which is a forward/backward movement. Some other figures are the Cross-over, Chase, Charge, Side break,.

On the "hold" count the feet remain together, side-by-side, although they need not be in exact alignment.

STRUCTURE OF THE MAMBO

PART A - BASIC CONDITIONS

THE NORMAL ACTION. The Manbo exemplifies the rapid steps and energetic body movement, especially of the hips, of Latino dances. Danced in a narrow space.

POSITION AT THE START.   May be danced in the closed position or apart.

TIME SIGNATURE.   4/4 time,   (cut- time 2/4 time).

TEMPO.   48 bars per minute.

PART B - PATTERN OF THE DANCE

READING DOWN EACH COLUMN:
   Col. 1: Practice the steps by walking, without music
   Col. 2: With music playing, put rhythm to the steps.
   Col. 3: Add duration of time to the steps.
   Col. 4: Add foot position to the steps.

THE MAMBO - Pattern for the Man

Pattern of the Steps	Rhythm Count	Step Time	Type Step
Hold this step, in place	1	Quick	Flat
LF forward	2	Quick	Flat
RF backward	3	Quick	Flat
LF close RF	4	Quick	Flat
Hold this step, in place	1	Quick	Flat
RF backward	2	Quick	Flat
LF forward	3	Quick	Flat
RF close LF	4	Quick	Flat

Total count: 1, 2, 3, 4,   5, 6, 7, 8.
Steps are flat to allow weight change and hip movement.

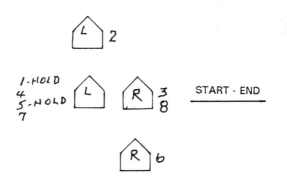

THE MAMBO - Pattern for the Lady

Pattern of the Steps	Rhythm Count	Step Time	Type Step
Hold in place	1	Quick	Flat
RF backward	2	Quick	Flat
LF forward	3	Quick	Flat
RF close LF	4	Quick	Flat
Hold in place	1	Quick	Flat
LF forward	2	Quick	Flat
RF backward	3	Quick	Flat
LF close RF	4	Quick	Flat

Total count: 1, 2, 3, 4,   5, 6, 7, 8.
Steps are flat to allow for weight change and hip movement.

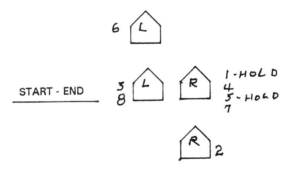

♪ ♪ ♪   DANCE NOTES   ♪ ♪ ♪

Chapter 17

The Samba

The Samba is pure Brazilian and is often called the national dance and dance of the people. It is sometimes called the Latin Polka and also the Bossa Nova.

The origin of the Samba is African and was imported to Brazil in the days of slavery. It became popular in the 1920's.

The Samba is a gay and lively dance with a rocking motion from side to side caused by the bending and straightening (flexing) of the knees. And this in turn emphasizes a hip motion that can be accentuated by the Cuban hip movement.

Most of the footwork in the Samba begins on the ball of the foot and then lowering the heel until the foot is flat although it is quite popular to perform the entire dance on the flat of the foot.

The basic movement is a forward / backward action and one of two rhythms may be used. First, a rhythmic count of 1 &, 2 &, 3 &, 4 &. Secondly, 1 & 2, 3 & 4. In our description below we shall use the second rhythmic count.

In the tables below we shall define three figures of the Samba: Forward / Backward, Chasse' and Box.

Some additional figures are: El Progresso, 5th position break, promenade, arch turn, overhead switch (arm slide), Corta Jaca, left and right turns.

STRUCTURE OF THE SAMBA

PART A - BASIC CONDITIONS

THE NORMAL ACTION.   The Samba is danced with all of the strong action of Latino dances but is more modified than the Mambo and Merengue. The couple keep turning to the man's right as the dance proceeds.

POSITION AT THE START. May be danced in the closed position or apart position.

TIME SIGNATURE.   2/4 time (4/4 split time).

TEMPO. Average 50 bar per minute.

ACCENT.   and 2.

PART B - PATTERN OF THE DANCE

READING DOWN EACH COLUMN:
    Col. 1 - Practice the steps by walking, without music.
    Col. 2 - With music playing, put rhythm to the steps.
    Col. 3 - Put duration of time to the steps.
    Col. 4 - Put foot position to the steps.

THE SAMBA - BASIC
Pattern for the Man

Pattern of the Steps	Rhythm Count	Step Time	Type Step
LF forward	1	Quick	Flat
RF close LF	&	Quick	Ball
LF step in place	2	Slow	Flat
RF backward	3	Quick	Flat
LF close RF	&	Quick	Ball
RF step in place	4	Slow	Flat

Total count: 1, 2, 3,   4, 5, 6.

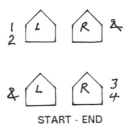

START - END

THE SAMBA - BASIC
Pattern for the Lady

Pattern of the Steps	Rhythm Count	Step Time	Type Step
RF backward	1	Quick	Flat
LF close RF	&	Quick	Ball
RF step in place	2	Slow	Flat
LF foreward	3	Quick	Flat
RF close LF	&	Quick	Ball
LF step in place	4	Slow	Flat

Total count: 1, 2, 3, 4, 5, 6.

START - END

THE SAMBA - CHASSE'
Pattern for the Man

Pattern of the Steps	Rhythm Count	Step Time	Type Step
LF to the side	1	Quick	Flat
RF close LF	&	Quick	Ball
LF step in plazce	2	Slow	Flat
RF to the side	3	Quick	Flat
LF close RF	&	Quick	Ball
RF step in place	4	Slow	Flat

Total count: 1, 2, 3,   4, 5, 6.

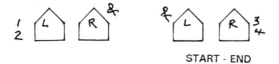

START - END

THE SAMBA - CHASSE'
Pattern for the Lady

Pattern of the Steps	Rhythm Count	Step Time	Type Step
RF to the side	1	Quick	Flat
LF close RF	&	Quick	Ball
RF step in place	2	Slow	Flat
LF to the side	3	Quick	Flat
RF close LF	&	Quick	Ball
LF step in place	4	Slow	Flat

Total count: 1, 2,3,   4, 5, 6.

START - END

THE SAMBA - BOX
Pattern for the Man

Pattern of the Steps	Rhythm Count	Step Time	Type Step
LF forward	1	Quick	Flat
RF to the side	&	Quick	Ball
LF close RF	2	Slow	Flat
RF backward	2	Quick	Flat
LF to the side	&	Quick	Ball
RF close LF	4	Slow	Flat

Total count: 1, 2, 3,   4, 5, 6.

START - END

THE SAMBA - BOX
Pattern for the Lady

Pattern of the Steps	Rhythm Count	Step Time	Type Step
RF backward	1	Quick	Flat
LF to the side	&	Quick	Ball
RF close LF	2	Slow	Flat
LF forward	3	Quick	Flat
RF to the side	&	Quick	Ball
LF close RF	4	Slow	Step

Total count: 1, 2, 3,   4, 5, 6.

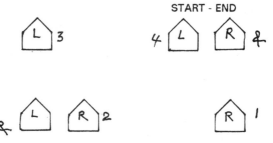

Chapter 18

The Disco

Disco dancing is not a single, particular dance such as we mean when we say Swing Dance or Tango Dance. Rather it is a style of dancing, a type of body movement on the dance floor that has its own particular manner of responding to the music.

Disco (or discotheque) became popular in the 1960's and 70's with a throbbing beat of music and a rhythmic movement involving the whole body, with much flexing of the knees.

Unlike most ballroom and Latin dancing, Disco does not have a set pattern in a sequence of steps, that is, it is not constructed to a set form of LF forward, RF forward, LF to the side, etc. Indeed, it is the very opposite of formal stepping for there is no prescribed formula to the routine. Disco is free-style in which the dancer improvises as he or she are performing the dance, as they respond to the music on the dance floor. This is the distinguishing character of Disco dancing.

Disco dancing is very much the slave of the music for it is the strong, pulsating beat, emphasized by loudness, that prompts the dancer to stomp, tap, pivot, dip, twist, turn and lean the torso in many directions. The music induces an elated feeling in the person who then expresses this feeling in a dance.

Disco dancing is set to rock type music and the dancer responds with agitated body movements as exhibited by Elvis Presley, although such extremes are usually not performed by the average Disco dancer on the dance floor. The normal dancer more often dances in a modified style, even a graceful manner, in response to the music. The rock and roll music of Bill Haley and the Comets might represent the norm for disco dancing.

Disco type dancing may be done with a partner in the closed position, with a partner in the apart position or solo (alone).

The time signature is 4/4 cut time, that is, 2/4 time.

The tempo is:
> 50 bars per minute, if danced to Quickstep music;
> 40 bars per minute if danced to Rock & Roll music.

Accent is (usually) assigned to all notes.

Rhythmic time approximates Q-Q-Q-Q-S-S.

In summary, Disco is a style, a type of dancing that has the character of strong musical beats with emphasized body movements of turns and twists, stomping and dips. While it is usually danced as an individual style, it may also be incorporated into Swing, Cha Cha and even Line dancing. A rough comparison might be the Samba danced to rock music

The tables below express a basic set of steps that are performed in disco dancing.

Follow the normal routine of first walking the steps without music until the pattern becomes familiar and then dance the steps with appropriate music playing.

BASIC DISCO

For the man.

Pattern of the Steps	Rhythm Count	Step Time	Type Step
LF Diagonal forward	1	Quick	Toe
LF close RF	2	Quick	Flat
RF diagonal forward	3	Quick	Toe
RF close LF	4	Quick	Flat
LF step in place	5	Slow	Flat
RF step in place	6	Slow	Flat

Steps 1 and 3 may be a kick forward instead of a toe touch.

START - END

BASIC DISCO

For the Lady.

Pattern of the Steps	Rhythm Count	Step Time	Type Step
RF backward	1	Quick	Toe
RF close LF	2	Quick	Flat
LF backward	3	Quick	Toe
LF close RF	4	Quick	Flat
RF step in place	5	Slow	Flat
LF step in place	6	Slow	Flat

Tempo is rapid.

START - END

Chapter 19

The Line Dance

As the name implies, line dancing is a line of people positioned side by side, and all dancing the same steps. And here we touch on the uniqueness of line dancing where one person alone (solo) may engage in the dance, or five people as a group may dance together or fifty-five people as a group may dance together. Prior to the appearance of line dancing a few decades ago the largest group of dancers performing together was eight, in the square dance. But with the coming of line dancing and large groups, the square dance seems like a tea party.

Line dancing is a style of dancing all its own, a category of dance that is separated by its unique patterns from such other categories as ballroom, Latin or folk dancing. But it is not entirely novel because it does incorporate many characteristics of the other dances such as polka, swing, cha cha, disco and even tango figures. Moreover the music carries a rhythmic beat similar to swing, modified rock and roll, Latin and two-step.

While line dancing is usually danced as or in a group, many persons prefer to dance the steps alone, solo. These people feel that they can express a freedom, an elation, a joy that is their very own. Here there is no need to regulate one's behavior to the whims of a partner nor to follow the dictates of a book of "rules of dancing."   Just dance as the spirit—or music—moves you!

One distinctive feature of line dancing deserves comment and that is the turning movement.   Many of the dances have this action of four quarter turns by the entire group.   It goes like this: In the starting position the group is facing the north wall.

First they do X number of steps and then turn left a quarter turn, now facing the west wall; again they do X number of steps, make a quarter turn left and now face the south wall; the process is repeated and they now face the east wall;   the process is repeated and they now face the north wall, having completed a 360 degree turn and ready to repeat the series. (See the Electric Slide below).

To condense the extensive subject of line dancing we shall enumerate the basic units, list a few of the dances, list some of the musical pieces and then define one dance, the Electric Slide, as an example.

BASIC UNITS OF LINE DANCING

•   Forward / Backward steps.
•   Chassee.   Moving sideways, left or right, without crossing the feet.
•   Vine Step (grapevine).   Stepping sideways by crossing one foot behind the other.
•   Cross Step (also called Jazz step).   Step sideways by crossing one foot in front of the other..
•   Tapping.   Extend the foot and tap the heel on the floor.
•   Triple step.   Three short steps forward: L - R - L.
•   Rock Step.   Extending one foot and rocking the body forward / backward, changing the body weight only.
•   Bunny Hop.   Jump forward with both feet, simultaneously.
•   Schottische.   A combination of three walking steps and a hop.

A FEW NAMED DANCES
- Electric Slide (a favorite)
- Honky Tonk Stomp
- Tush Push
- Ski Bumpus (a favorite)
- Achy Breaky Heart
- Cotton Eyed Joe
- Boot Scootin' Boogie
- Watermelon Crawl
- Cowboy Cha Cha

SOME MUSICAL PIECES
- Elvira
- Pecos Push
- Achy Breaky Heart
- The Squeeze
- Ropeville
- Hot Footing'
- Pink Cadillac
- Seminole Stroll

STRUCTURE OF THE ELECTRIC SLIDE

PART A - BASIC CONDITIONS

THE NORMAL ACTION.   An average line dance.

POSITION AT START.   Group in line, side by side.

TIME SIGNATURE.   4/4 time.

TEMPO.   Moderate, 30 bars per minute.

PART B - PATTERN OF THE DANCE

READING DOWN EACH COLUMN:
Col 1:   Practice the steps without music.
Col. 2:   With music playing, put rhythm to the steps.
Col. 3:   Add duration of time to the steps.
Col. 4:   Add foot position to the steps.

ELECTRIC SLIDE

Pattern for Man and Lady

Pattern of the Steps	Total Count	Step Time	Type Step
UNIT ONE			
RF to the side	1	Quick	Flat
LF cross behind RF	2	Quick	Flat
RF to side	3	Quick	Flat
LF close to RF	4	Quick	Toe
LF to the side	5	Quick	Flat
RF cross behind LF	6	Quick	Flat
LF to the side	7	Quick	Flat
RF close to LF	8	Quick	Toe
RF backward	9	Quick	Flat
Rock forward on LF	10	Quick	Flat
Rock back on RF	11	Quick	Flat
Rock forward on LF	12	Quick	Flat
UNIT TWO			
RF forward and turn left 90 degrees	13	Quick	Flat
Repeat steps 2 - 12	14-24		
UNIT THREE			
Repeat unit two.	25-36		
UNIT FOUR			
Repeat unit two.	37-48		

The rhythmic count is 1, 2, 3, 4 • 1, 2, 3, 4 • 1, 2, 3, 4.,

Unit One - Start by facing wall #1.

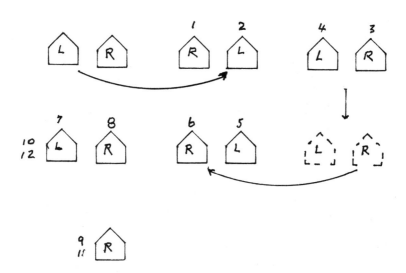

Unit Two - Turn to face wall #2

Count 13 - RF forward and turn left 90 degreees.
Repeat steps 2 - 12.

Unit Three - Turn to face wall #3.

Repeat Unit Two.

Unit Four - Turn to face wall #4.

Repeat Unit Two.

Chapter 20

American Folk Dances

If we take the term"folk dance" in its strict meaning of a dance that is native to a particular place or people such as the German Polka or the Scottish Sword Dance, then the United States has no original folk dance. If we take the meaning to be a dance that has been performed for many years, beginning with the early settlers, then we may establish three American Folk Dances: the Square Dance, the Contra Dance and the Round Dance. However, even these were imported from the British Isles from whence the original settlers came but they have been modified with the passing of time and events until today they do have an American flavor or style.

THE SQUARE DANCE

Without doubt the square dance has been the most popular of the folk dances down through the decades of American history and it is pursued today as vigorously as in the past. One ingredient that has sustained the square dance is its adaptability to the American environment. When the eastern seaboard was the entirety of the United States, in the 1700's, with a frontier condition and an agricultural economy, that is to say a "countrified" population, the square dance was well suited to the times.   Then, as the people moved westward for 200 years and thus still lived in a "country" (rural) condition, the square dance was the major social participation of the people. The   "dance down at the school house" or even around the camp fire provided high recreation and social association.

The square dance is a quadrille formation with four couples forming a square, one couple on each side of the square and this is their home position. The couples perform all of their dance within this square: forward and backward steps, turns and circles, dancing as a couple and with exchange of partners from another couple.

The step movements are quite simple, being a walking action with no scuffing of feet or triple stepping.   The arms are not held in unusual positions or waved in exhibition.   The torso is held erect with no contortions.

The square dance has a caller, that is, a person who calls out the movements to be made by the couples He (or she) coordinate the figures that the couples perform and also induce a joyful, happy atmosphere for all of the persons on the floor and the spectators, too.

There are three types of calls:

1)   A prompting call. In a firm   voice the caller gives directions to the dancers so that they "march up the center and cut-off two," "do-se-do" or "swing your partner."   The caller keeps about two beats ahead of the dancers so that they know the proper steps to take in time with the music.

2) Singing. This call employs a singing of the commands in tune with the music.   The dancers must be thoroughly acquainted with the directions in order to complete the dance in order and not in confusion.

3)   Patter. Similar to the singing call and again the dancers must be experienced and know their business.

The condition that infuses order into the dance is the numbering of the couples. The system works like this: When the couples form-up at the beginning of the dance, the couple with their backs to the caller or the orchestra is known as the first couple; the second couple is the two persons to the right of couple #1; the third couple is the two persons to the right of couple #2; the fourth couple is the two persons to the right of couple #3. Accordingly, when the caller commands that the "first couple" will do so-and-so or the "second couple" will do this-and-that, the designated couple will dance the figures commanded.

Time for the square dance is 4/4 or 6/8 time.

The tempo is moderate, about 38 to 40 bars per minute.

Some familiar music is:

Turkey in the Straw	Arkansas Traveler
Pop goes the Weasel	Little Brown Jug
Alabama Jubilee	Oh, Susannah
Comin' 'Round the Mountain	

THE CONTRA DANCE

In the contra dance the couples line-up as the name implies—contra to each other—in two lines facing each other, in two parallel lines. Each couple will then step forward, perform a dance figure and then return to the line. In the southern United States this dance is also called the Virginia Reel.

Some well-known tunes: Maple Leaf Jig, Pop Goes the Weasel, Haymakers Jig.

THE ROUND DANCE

The Round Dance is quite popular in some areas of the country. This is a couples dance and it is "round" because of the formation of the couples. Before the dancing starts the couples lineup and form a large circle around the entire dance floor. When the music starts each couple will dance one figure in a small area, then move forward in a CCW direction as they are dancing another figure, then pause and dance a figure in a small area, and again move forward. This pausing and then moving forward presents the image of a large circle in motion.

Like the square dance, the round dance also has a caller but in the round dance he (or she) is known as a cue-er, he cues the dancers. Having a caller for the dance, every couple on the floor will be dancing the same figures, taking the same steps, all at the same time.

Some well known figures that are danced are the waltz, polka, two-step, rumba, samba and merengue. The cue-er, in commanding the dancers to perform these figures, will call the steps such as: vine step, walk step, chasse', cross step, etc.

Some well-known tunes of the round dance are Portland Fancy, Patty-Cake, Circassin Circle.

SUPPLEMENT

In this supplement we shall examine several dances in syllabus form, that is, in a summary of the main points. These dances are no less important than those described in the several chapters but they are less widely known and danced, even though most dance instructors include these dances as part of their choreography instructions. In other words, these dances appeal to a limited public.

Another point to be noted is the fact that such dances as the Hustle and Country-Western are not distinct types of dances, not separate forms of the dance, rather they are a type of dance that incorporates, that are a blend of such dances as the swing, disco and line dances. They are merely a different slant of other dances that have been long established.

In this supplement we shall briefly review six dances and to clarify their position in the whole scheme of dancing, (and thus supplement Chapter 6), we shall again sail out into the choppy waters of classifying dances and in particular the so-called "social dances."

SOCIAL DANCES

Stated in approximation there are six classes of social dances. These are, with examples:

BALLROOM—Waltz, Foxtrot, Swing, Polka.

LATIN—Tango, Cha Cha, Rumba.

LATINO—Samba, Mambo, Merengue.

LINE DANCE—Same steps as in Ballroom and Latin dances but the formation of the dancers is in-line by individuals instead of partner dancing in closed or apart positions.

DISCO—Disco dancing is characterized by excessive movement of the limbs and contortions of the torso as the dancer responds to the loud and heavy beats of Rock and Roll music.

AMERICAN FOLK DANCES—Square, Round, Contra.

SIX ADDITIONAL DANCE STYLES—the following, below.

COUNTRY - WESTERN DANCE

The tern "country - western" is a combing of two entities
1) Country Dance refers to the early styles of dancing, say down to 1920, such as the square and round dances. They were held in the "country" meaning a rural area, away from cities, where "country folks" lived.
2) Western of course refers to the western part of the United States, say west of the Mississippi River.
So it is confusing to say "country - western" dance, yet the term persists—and—is a favorite dance in the big cities of today.
Then, to add to the confusion, when we examine the type of dances the"country - western" dancers do, we find that there

is no square dancing but on the contrary swing steps, line dance, foxtrot and disco.   That which makes the dance "western" is the cowboy attire that is worn by the dancers.

The action in Country - Western Dancing is lively, vigorous and sharp.

Time signature is 4 / 4 time or 2 / 4 split time.

Tempo may be moderate or fast, about 40 bars per minute.

Rhythm Count may be 1, 2, 3, 4 or 1, 2, 3-a, 4.

Foot steps will then be straight or syncopated, thus:

    1,   2,   3-a,   4
    Q,   Q,   Slow,   Q

Some Country - Western dance patterns:

| Two Step | Schottische | Bunny Hop |
| Pasadena Polka | Cotton Eyed Joe | Waltz |

THE HUSTLE

The Hustle became popular in the mid-1970's. It is not a new or separate kind of dancing, rather it is shoot-off from disco dancing, a stylized disco. The Hustle embodies all of the steps of swing, cha cha, foxtrot and polka but it executes these patterns in a different manner. Where the former pattern or steps are done with smoothness and grace, in Hustle the movement is more in the fashion of disco, being more lively.

The Hustle is danced both in closed and apart position, some times alternating in the same dance, that is, danced for a while in closed position, then danced in apart position and then return to the closed position.

Time signature is 4 / 4, 2 / 4 cut time.

Tempo: the average is 45 beats per minute.

Counting may be straight 1, 2, 3; or syncopated 1, 2, a 3, as in Latin Hustle.

.The basic pattern in straight count is thus:

LF - point toe to the left.	Q
LF - close to RF.	Q
RF - point toe to the right.	Q
RF - close to LF.	Q
LF - step in place.	Q
RF - step in place	Q

Total of six counts.

THE LATIN HUSTLE

The Latin Hustle is similar to the Basic Hustle as to time, tempo and action but the step pattern is different because it contains a   syncopated beat, shown below. Hip action is prominent and the apart position is preferred.

Basic Hustle: 1,   2,   3,   1, 2 ,   3,   etc

Latin Hustle: 1, 2-a,   3,   4, 5-a,   6.

LATIN HUSTLE - For the man.

Pattern of Steps	Rhythm Count	Step Time	Type Step
Touch LF diag. Fwd.	1	Q	Toe
LF close RF	2	Q	Flat
RF step Backwd	a		Ball
LF step in Place	3	S	Flat
RF kick Fwd	4	Q	Kick
RF Backward	5	Q	Flat
LF step in Place	a		Ball
RF close LF	6	S	Flat

Latin Hustle pattern)

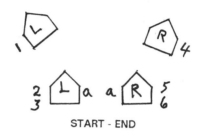

START - END

THE QUICKSTEP

The Quickstep is derived from the one-step and came into being in the first decade of the 20th Century.

The Quickstep is danced in the closed position to moderately fast music.

The action is similar to that of the Foxtrot with the fundamental movements of a walk and a chasse'. The walks are forward and backward, the chasse' to left and right. And the chasse', as always, is a 3-step count of Q - Q - S, four beats of music.

The time signature is 4 / 4, 2 / 4 split time.

The tempo is 50 to 52 bars per minute.

Steps include the quarter turns, progressive chasse', fish tail, lock step backward, running right turn.

Two foot counts are used: (1), S-Q-Q-S-S, and

(2), S-S-Q-Q-S. The latter sequence is the most popular for lively music.

QUICKSTEP SEQUENCE FOR THE MAN

LF Forward	1	S
RF Forward	2	S
LF Forward	3	Q
RF Forward	&	Q
LF Forward	4	S
RF Forward	5	S
LF Forward	6	S
RF Forward	7	Q
LF Forward	&	Q
RF Forward	8	S

Total of 8 counts.

PASO DOBLE

The Paso Doble is a Spanish dance and the movements of the dancers depict or are symbolic of the bull fight. in which the man is the torero (matador) who torments the bull and the lady represents the cape passes that take place during a bull fight. The term"paso doble" means two step.

The music is lively and sharp, played 2/4 or 6/8 time,which is march tempo. In this dance the tempo is 62 bars per minute.

The Paso Doble is a dramatic and spectacular dance, fast, sharp, precise. It became popular in the north in the 1930's.

The beat value is one step for each beat in 2/4 time and one step for each three beats of music in 6/8 time.

Dance titles include the Sur Place, The Huit (eight), The Appel, the Promenade Link.

BOSSA NOVA

The Bossa Nova is a musical form that originated in Brazil and then modified into a jazzy Samba music for modern dancing.

The Bossa Nova is also a couples dance and the figures are quite similar to the Samba Dance patterns.

THE BOLERO

This is largly a theatrical dance but a modified version or revised version appeared in the late 18th century for social dancing, for couples dancing.

Glossary

accent   The notes in a measure that are   emphasized by loudness   or duration.

alignment   Body posture while standing straight. A plumb line that is held before the ear and dropping down past the shoulder, hip, knee and ankle.

apart position   No contact between partners while dancing.

ball-change   This is a term that comes from Tap Dancing and it means a quick change of body weight, of shifting the weight from one foot to another foot very quickly. There are two kinds of ball-change:
1) Step ball-change means the usual change of weight from the ball of one foot to the ball of another foot in the course of dancing.
2) Kick ball-change mens to make the change when a kick is made.
These changes usually match the syncopated count of "a" or "and" and take place at that time.

ballroom dance   A dance that is performed in a ballroom or dance hall and is variously known as   partner dancing, touch   dancing and couple dancing.

basic   A foundational pattern or figure of a dance, a pattern from which other patterns are copied.

broken rhythm   A series of slow or quick beats that extend across more than one measure; an uneven series of rhythmic beats; syncopated beats..

chasse'   A gliding dance step sideways; two steps in any direction.   The second step is a closing step to the first one. (LF to the left, RF closes to LF).

close   To bring the feet together.

counting   There are two kinds of counting in dancing. rhythm counting and step counting. This is so because you cannot change the beat of the music but you can take two or three steps to one beat. The foxtrot is 4/4 time and a four-step count; the single swing is 4/4 time and a six-step count; the triple swing is 4/4 time and an eight count time (two triple steps).

cut time   This means that the half note is the basic unit of time, not the quarter note. Thus where the time is written as 4/4 and the cut symbol is inserted, the first two notes are played as the first beat and the last two notes are played   as the second beat. Thus:

As 4/4 time, count 1, 2, 3, 4,   1, 2, 3, 4, etc

As cut time, count   1, 2   1, 2   etc.

cross over   A cross over is the partners turning to the side from the forward / backward movement and executing a step, as in the cha cha, when they turn east and do a rock step then turn west and do another rock step.

Cuban hip movement   To cause the hip to protrude by flexing (bending) the knee—flex the left knee and the right hip will protrude; flex the right knee and the left hip will protrude.

dance space   (1) There are three progressive dances in which the dancers move constantly CCW around the dance floor and these are the foxtrot, waltz and tango. (2)   All other dances are   performed   in a close area such as the swing, cha cha, polka, rumba, mambo.

dance, starting   In America, all dances start with the man stepping forward with his left foot and the lady stepping backward with her right foot.

dance standards   Standards refer to the levels of skill that a dancer may acquire.   These levels are set by the International Dance Council and the American Dance Council and they apply to each particular dance such as the tango, swing (jive), cha cha, rumba, etc. A common classification is bronze, silver and gold to indicate an ascending level of skill. (See page 8)..

double time   Means two steps in two beats as in a walk step, chasse' step and rock step.

down beat   The first beat of a measure.

even rhythm   A steady, consistent beat in each measure of the music, each with the same time value (such as all quarter notes).

fall-away position   A couple traveling backward, in promenade position.

figure   A series of steps within a dance pattern; a sub-pattern within a whole pattern.

free foot   The foot that has no weight on it..

hand position   see chapter 5.

inside foot   The foot nearest your partner.

kick   Kick means a lifting of the foot or a small flick of t h e foot forward, to the side or backward. It does not mean b fling the foot far out from the body, (as in a chorus line), which is a dangerous act on a crowded dance floor.

line dance   A style of dancing, see Chapter 19.

line of direction   The line of direction or line of dance (LOD) is the flow of traffic around the dance floor, in a counter-clockwise direction (CCW).

lock step   A group of three steps. When dancing forward the second step is crossed behind the first step; when moving backward the second step is crossed in front of the first step.

locomotor movements   The actions that move a dancer from one point to another as we see in the walk step, jump, run, hop and slide steps.

measure   A division of music into equal groups of notes, equal beats, and shown by vertical lines on a staff; also, a stately dance.

open position   Dancing when bodies are apart but hands are being held.

overhead switch   or the arm slide   From the closed position the couple will each step slightly to the left to form the outside position, side by side, still holding hands and facing in opposite directions.   Couple then raise their held hands and place them behind each others head.   Couple now release their held hands, step away from each other and as they part for several beats   the man's right   hand slides down the lady's right arm and the lady's right hand   slides down the man's right arm. When their hands meet they return to   the closed position.

pattern   (of a dance)   The basic configurations of a dance such as the waltz or the tango; the basic series of steps in a dance.   Variations of this basic structure are designated as figures, that is,   sub-patterns.

phrase   Two or more measures of music grouped together.

pivot   To swivel or turn on the ball of the foot.

position   The place of each partner in dancing. (See chapter 5).

preparatory or lead-in step   A step taken before the   normal pattern of a dance begins. (See chapter 13, the Cha Cha).

progressive dances   The foxtrot, tango and waltz are usually designated as the progressive dances because the couple move   over a large area of the dance floor.   All other dances are designated as   small area dances.

quick step   In musical terms, quick means a tempo of 40 or more measures per minute and "slow" means a tempo below 40 bars per minute. This standard has been set by the International Dance Council.

In dance terms, "quick" means a duration of time to the step equal to one beat of music. "Slow" equals two beats of music.

Or, stated otherwise, "slow" equals two beats of music and also two quick steps.

rhythm patterns Rhythm means a recurring of events such as the sun rising every morning or the tides rising and falling. In music, rhythm means a group of notes that recur over and over on a musical staff and are set apart into groups called measures or bars. In playing the notes some are strong and some are weak, that is, heavily or lightly accented and hence emitting a rhythmic pattern, a recurring pattern. In dancing, this rhythm is interpreted as foot steps of which there are patterns:

1) Single rhythm—1 step in 2 beats (foxtrot, tango).

2) Double rhythm—2 steps in 2 beats (waltz, walk, chasse').

3) Triple rhythm—3 steps in 2 beats (triple swing, cha cha).

rock step One foot is stepped forward and the torso "rocks" forward putting weight on the forward foot and then body rocks backward putting weight in the back foot. Performed in cha cha and swing dancing.

salsa A Latino dance; Latin dance.

Schottische This is an European folk dance, set to 4/4 time. It is a lively dance and can be dance as a round dance with a partner or as a line dance. Here is one pattern (the man):

1. LF forward.
2. RF crosses back of LF
3. Swing LF back to closed position beside RF.
4. Kick RF outward.

5. Step RF back to the floor, close to LF.
6. Cross LF back of RF.
7. Swing RF back to closed position beside LF.
8. Kick LF outward.

social dance   An individual or couple dancing for recreational reasons; any gathering of persons who engage in dancing as friends and associates.

spot dance   A dance pattern performed within a small area of the dance floor as opposed to a "traveling" dance around the LOD.

starting to dance   This is something of a formality in all dances.   A couple will go to the edge of the dance floor and then step on to the floor together and assume their position either closed, apart, in-line, etc. They will pause for a bit to catch the rhythm of the music and then begin dancing.

step in place   Lift the foot and then place it back on the floor in the same place without taking a step in any direction.

step in tune   A square dance expression meaning "step to the tune" of the music and—of the caller.

supporting foot   The foot with the body weight on it.

tempo   The speed of the music and therefore of the dance.   It is expressed as so many measures (bars) per minute: the waltz has 30 MPM,   the polka 58 MPM, the tango 31 MPM.

time signature   This denotes the time value of the notes both in duration (whole, half, quarter notes) and number of beats in a measure.   This double quantity is expressed in a fractional symbol thusly: 3 / 4 time tells by the numerator 3 that there are three beats in each measure (bar) and the denominator 4 tells that the value of each note is one-quarter.

triple step(s)   Three steps in two beats of music. The British express it well with "three linked steps."

turns   See page 30, Dancing Turns.

two step   A step to each beat in 4 / 4 time.   In the Texas two-step the progression is this: Q-Q-S: 1,   2,   3-&-4,   5, 6, 7 & 8.

uneven rhythm   A combination of whole and half counts in a recurring series.

upbeat   The last beat of a measure which is often called an "and" count when one starts to dance with the music.

vine step   When stepping to the side,   one foot is crossed behind the other foot.

walk step   A forward or backward progression on the flat of the foot, as in normal walking.

♪　♪　♪　　DANCE　NOTES　　♪　♪　♪

Appendix

In this appendix we shall further examine the relationship of dancing to music. In particular we shall review note values, musical beat and count, and duration of foot steps. The purpose is to provide a quick reference guide for each type of dancing, although there is some redundancy.

Dancing is performed to the music that is written in the bass clef, not the treble clef. While the beautiful tones of music come from the treble clef, dancing is done from the bass clef, from the beat of the music.

This is the sign of the bass clef on the staff of five lines:

These are the five musical notes found in most dance music. Most of the steps in popular dancing are performed to the three middle notes:

A measure is the notes contained within the two bold bars on the staff, thus:

Recall that beats and counts are expressed *per measure*. Thus 3/4 time means three beats per measure and 4/4 time means four to the measure. The top number shows the number of beats, the bottom number indicates the value of the beat. These note values are not clock-time values, they are relative values. Thus a 1/4 note has the same value as two eighth notes.

CUT-TIME

In most popular music the basic unit of time, (note time) is the quarter note. But the music is usually written in cut-time, in which the basic unit of time is half of quarter time. It is equal to 2 / 4 time so that in each measure the first two quarter notes equal one beat and the last two quarter notes equal one beat, or, two beats per measure.

The time signature for cut-time is ¢ .

In some dance figures such as foxtrot and samba, the number of counts is the same as the number of beats per measure. In other figures such as swing and rumba, one beat equals two step counts.

TABLES OF TIME AND TEMPO

Note 1: In each table the last four columns represent a measure.
    a. First row is the beat.
    b. The second row is the rhythm count.
    c. The third row is the foot step relating to the note value.
Note 2: These tables have approximated values because dance structures vary by the teacher, the dance group, the territory (east, west, north and south) and official bodies.

THE CHA CHA   Time: 4 /4   Tempo 32 MPM

Beats	1	2	3	4
Count	1	2	3 &	4
Steps	S	S	Q Q	S

DISCO   Time: 4/4 (cut)   Tempo: 40 to 50 MPM

Beats	1	2	3	4
Count	1 &	2 &	3	4
Steps	Q Q	Q Q	S	S

FOXTROT   Time: 4/4   Tempo: 32 MPM

Beats	1	2	3	4
Count	1 &	2 &	3	4
Steps	S	S	Q	Q

MAMBO   Time 4/4, cut time   Tempo: 48 MPM

Beats	1	2	3	4
Count	Hold	2	3	4
Steps	Q	Q	Q	Q

MERENGUE   Time: 4/4 (cut time)   Tempo: 50 MPM

Beats	1	2	3	4
Count	1	2	3	&
Steps	Q	Q	S	

POLKA   Time: 4/4 cut time   Tempo: 44 - 48 MPM

Beats	1	2	3	4
Count	1 a	2	3 a	4
Steps	Q Q	S	Q Q	S

ROCK & ROLL   Time: 4/4 cut time   Tempo: 40 MPM

Beats	1	2	3	4
Count	1 &	2 &	3	4
Steps	S	S	Q	Q

RUMBA   Time: 4/4   Tempo: 27 - 32 MPM

Beats	1	2	3	4
Counts	1, 2	3	4, 5	6
Steps	Q Q	S	Q Q	S

SAMBA Time: 4/4 cut time Tempo: 50 - 54 MPM

Beats	1	2	3	4
Count	1&	2	3 &	4
Steps	Q Q	S	Q Q	S

SINGLE SWING Time: 4/4 cut time Tempo: 44 MPM

Beats	1	2	3	4
Count	1 &	2 &	3	4
Steps	S	S	Q	Q

TANGO Time: 4/4 Tempo: 31 - 33 MPM

Beats	1	2	3	4
Count	1 - 2	3 - 4	5 - 6	7 -8
Steps	S	S	S	Q Q

TRIPLE SWING Time: 4/4 cut time Tempo: 40 MPM

Beats	1	2	3	4
Count	1 & 2	3 & 4	5	6
Steps	Q Q S	Q Q S	Q	Q

TWO-STEP   Time: 4/4 cut time.   Tempo: 44-MPM

Beats	1	2	3	4
Count	1	2	3 &	
Steps	Q	Q	S	

WALTZ   Time: 3/4   Tempo   30 MPM

Beats	1	2	3	
Count	1 &	2	3	
Steps	S	Q	Q	

♪ ♪ ♪ DANCE NOTES ♪ ♪ ♪

♪　　♪　　♪　　DANCE　NOTES　　♪　　♪　　♪

♪   ♪   ♪   DANCE NOTES   ♪   ♪   ♪

♪   ♪   ♪   DANCE NOTES   ♪   ♪   ♪